Between Sundays

A YEAR of TRANSFORMING DEVOTIONALS

for the TOUGHEST DAYS of the WEEK

HOWARD BOOKS
A DIVISION OF SIMON & SCHUSTER
New York   London   Toronto   Sydney

SHAWN CRAIG

Shawn Craig is the middle name in Phillips, Craig, and Dean (PCD), one of the most popular contemporary Christian music groups in the world today. A prolific songwriter, Shawn has had many of his songs recorded by artists such as Point of Grace, the Gaither Vocal Band, and Glen Campbell. He has received two Dove awards, including the 1994 Song of the Year "In Christ Alone," and several Dove nominations. Shawn currently serves as the Senior Pastor at South County Christian Center where he has ministered for the past twenty-six years in various roles of music ministry, worship leading, and Bible teaching. Shawn has earned a Bachelor of Arts degree from Webster University in St. Louis, and in 2005, a Masters of Divinity Degree at Oral Roberts University in Tulsa, Oklahoma.

For more information about Shawn Craig of Phillips, Craig, and Dean, contact: PhillipsCraigAndDean.com.

To my

mom and *dad*,

Ted and Beverly Craig,

who, in between,
live what they profess on Sundays

Our purpose at Howard Books is to:
- Increase faith in the hearts of growing Christians
- Inspire holiness in the lives of believers
- Instill hope in the hearts of struggling people everywhere

Because He's coming again!

Howard Books, a division of Simon & Schuster, Inc.
1230 Avenue of the Americas, New York, NY 10020
www.howardpublishing.com

Between Sundays © 2006 by Shawn Craig

Library of Congress Cataloging-in-Publication Data

Craig, Shawn, 1959-
    Between Sundays / Shawn Craig. — Rev. & adapted from earlier version.
        p. cm.
    ISBN-13: 978-1-4165-3803-5; ISBN-10: 1-4165-3803-8
    ISBN-13: 978-1-58229-67; ISBN-10: 1-58229-675-8
    1. Devotional calendars. I. Title.

BV4811.C687 2007
242'.2—dc22

2006049610

10 9 8 7 6 5 4 3 2 1

HOWARD colophon is a registered trademark of Simon & Schuster, Inc.
Manufactured in the United States of America
For information regarding special discounts for bulk purchases, please contact Simon & Schuster Special Sales at 1-800-456-6798 or business@simonandschuster.com.

Edited by Sue Ann Jones
Cover design by John Lucas
Interior design by Tennille Paden

Acknowledgments

*I*n order for this dream to become reality, there have been many wonderful people who have made invaluable contributions. My thanks go out to . . .

Philis and the editorial staff at Howard Books for their patience and hard work through this whole process,

Joy Becker for encouraging me to keep writing,

Demie Rainey for her insight and editorial pointers along the way,

Pastor Gerald and my church family for loving me and allowing me time to write and sing and be gone days at a time,

Dave, Kim, and the music team for their faithfulness and understanding,

Pamela Muse for introducing me to Howard Books, and

Randy Phillips and Dan Dean for helping me to remember to laugh more often.

INTRODUCTION

*T*he wise man said, "There is nothing new under the sun" (Ecclesiastes 1:9).

I once heard a pastor who related how excited he had been on having received what he thought was a new revelation on the subject he was preparing to preach about. But as he was reading a book in his own library, he discovered his "revelation" right there in chapter 1. Not only that, he had underlined it!

This book contains nothing new. It is the overflow of what so many have poured into me over the years through books I have read and God's wonderful people whom I have met.

This book began as a personal project as I journaled what I felt God was saying to me along my own journey of faith. But as a result of encouragement from friends, I began to put some of these thoughts into book form. It was my desire to have something I could give to younger Christians to encourage them to press on to know God more intimately and to find that Jesus is truly there between Sundays.

The reader may notice that the pronouns for God are not capitalized. This is not meant to show any disrespect to our mighty God but was a mutual decision between the editor and myself regarding a particular style of writing. It may be well noted that most editions of the King James Version as well as the New International Version do not capitalize divine pronouns.

A Moment of Reckoning

But you, lazybones, how long will you sleep? When will you wake up?—Proverbs 6:9 NLT

We don't always recognize a wake-up call when it happens. Only later do we realize that God was trying to shake us loose from the shackles of slumber.

Peter the apostle underwent a wake-up call. In the warmth of fellowship among his ministry peers at the Last Supper, he was quick to say, "Lord, I am ready to go with thee, both into prison, and to death" (Luke 22:33 KJV). But later, feeling the fire of scrutiny, he hastily denied any knowledge of Christ. Then, when he realized what he'd done and admitted how weak he truly was, his heart was broken, and a conversion took place.

God cannot fully use those who are totally self-reliant. It is from the broken places of our lives that we minister most effectively. In utter hopelessness we realize how much we desperately need God. Only then are we emboldened to do what is beyond ourselves, because only then do we realize our strength is from God and not something we can conjure up ourselves.

So when your faith is shaken or your world is suddenly turned upside down, stop and listen. It might be God's alarm clock going off in your life. Your wake-up call. Arise and shine; resist the snooze button.

Lord Jesus, let me recognize the crucial moments of my existence. Make me attentive to your workings, to your voice, and your purpose.

Stand by Me

He lifted me out of the slimy pit . . . ; he set my feet on a rock and gave me a firm place to stand.—*Psalm 40:2*

There on the mountaintop, Moses was so close to God, he could feel the holy light permeating his being as God's finger chiseled out the holy commandments for Israel.

"God, show me your glory," Moses said bravely.

God must have smiled, knowing his servant only too well. "There is a place near me where you may stand on a rock" (Exodus 33:21), God said. "I will cause all my goodness to pass in front of you" (Exodus 33:19).

As God's glory passed by, God covered Moses with his hand so his faithful servant got only a glimpse. Still, Moses's face shone for many days to come.

Later, in the last few days of his life, Moses was once again on the mountain. This time he had not come to view God's glory but to behold from afar the land of promise, land he could never obtain because of his disobedience. But once again he was not alone. He was with his friend, his God.

Whether we are basking in God's glory, facing disappointment, or confronting the truth of our transgressions, God is with us, helping us not to be afraid. He will cover with his hand what he knows we cannot bear. And he will give us the courage we need to encounter what we must.

Father, how I love to stand firmly beside you on that rock where you give me hope, strength, and courage to face whatever comes.

An Encounter with God

When they saw [their] courage . . . , they took note that these men had been with Jesus.—Acts 4:13

When I was asked recently which three people have had the greatest impact on my life, it wasn't easy to give an answer. I've encountered many, many helpers and mentors along the way who have impacted my life in varying ways, large and small. I couldn't name just three.

If someone asked me to identify the single source of life-changing impact in my life, however, I could answer immediately. The answer is God.

God's impact on his children's lives goes beyond the normal "bumping into" changes brought about by earthly helpers or motivators. When Moses met with God on Mount Sinai, God's glory shone so radiantly on Moses's face that he had to wear a veil later to address the Israelites. When Saul, the terrible persecutor of Christians, encountered God on the road to Damascus, he became the mighty apostle Paul, who would write more of the New Testament than any other disciple. Consider the stories of Abraham, Peter, Mary Magdalene, and all the others whose lives were radically changed after their date with divinity.

When we encounter God and allow him to change us, the transformation will be noticeable. Others will look at us and say we've never been the same since that moment.

Lord, please make your transformation of my life so evident that others notice and want their own encounter with you.

The Moment of Revelation

*Then their eyes were opened and they recognized him, and he
disappeared from their sight.*—*Luke 24:31*

Christ longs for us to open the doors of our hearts, to open our spiritual eyes so he can come in and reveal his heart, character, and love to us.

Two disciples met Jesus on their way to Emmaus but didn't recognize him because they were spiritually blinded. They spilled out their grief over the loss of their Master and Friend when the risen Lord was right there with them. Only later, as he blessed and broke the bread for them, did they suddenly recognize him. And then he was gone.

When Jesus comes into our lives and "breaks bread" by sharing his words of spirit and life, the blinders fall from our eyes. Maybe then he vanishes from our spiritual sight, not because he plays games, but because we can only receive revelation in small doses. In essence, we can only eat so much bread at one sitting!

As we wait and listen, we will hear his voice calling. If we will open the door, he will come in. He has said, "Whoever has my commands and obeys them, he is the one who loves me. He who loves me will be loved by my Father, and I too will love him and show myself to him" (John 14:21). If you love him, listen . . .

*Dear Lord, I will open the door of my heart to your revelation.
My knowledge of you will grow as I partake
of the Bread of Life.*

A Humbling Experience

*[Jesus] made himself nothing, taking the very nature of a servant
. . . in human likeness.—Philippians 2:7*

How humbling it must have been for God to become human and feel all the discomforts that were so different from his glorious existence in heaven. But that was only the beginning. Those difficulties couldn't compare with the humiliation he suffered on the cross, dying the most horrifying of deaths, experiencing complete rejection by the very ones he had come to save.

Today, despite all he's already done for us, he continues to humble himself, coming down to our level of understanding to meet us at our point of need. I love how Jack Deere, a former associate professor at Dallas Theological Seminary, tells how God met him at his level of faith. Jack was convinced that the miraculous was a thing of the past. But in his book *Surprised by the Power of the Spirit*, Jack explains how God patiently convinced him otherwise. Jack is a cerebral theologian, and he found that God was merciful enough to meet him at that level of understanding.

There will always be diversity in the body of Christ. One church will respond one way, while another will respond in a radically different manner. God is big enough, and yet humble enough, to understand both.

*Jesus, I want to remember your humility and your willingness
to be a servant and to make allowances for diversity
in my spiritual family.*

Weekend Reflections

God surprises us. He rarely shows up where and how we expect him to. When a Bible-study leader recently encouraged my group to spend a week looking for Jesus in those around us, I was amazed how we could see evidence of him in friends, family members, coworkers, and even strangers. When our minds are tuned to the idea and we actively look for him everywhere we go, we find the Savior in some surprising places (and people).

Pay attention! Jesus may pay you a surprise visit today through someone who touches your life.

Ripples of Reflection

- Why do you think the two disciples on the road to Emmaus didn't recognize Jesus? How does this apply to your situation?

- When and where do you find that you are most aware of Jesus? On Sundays in church? On a quiet night gazing at the stars? Watch for him, and you may find him in surprising places.

The Call to Remember

Consider your own call . . . : not many of you were wise . . . ,
[or] of noble birth.—1 Corinthians 1:26 NRSV

I love the word *remember*. It literally means to bring the picture back to your mind. The apostle Paul wanted the Corinthians to have the proper attitude of mind and spirit. So, in essence, he was saying, "When you are tempted to boast, remember your humble beginnings. Remember who you were before Christ found you." In the same way, Moses told the Israelites, "Remember that you were slaves in Egypt and that the LORD your God brought you out of there with a mighty hand and an outstretched arm" (Deuteronomy 5:15).

Remembering empowers us to move forward. Woodrow Wilson said, "A nation which does not remember what it was yesterday does not know what it is today, nor what it is trying to do. We are trying to do a futile thing if we do not know where we came from or what we have been about."

Remembering our calling and who we were before Christ found us does two things: it causes us to boast in the Lord instead of in ourselves, and it gives us faith in the mighty power of God. Remembering, we can boldly stand and say, "Christ saves! Christ delivers!" because we are living witnesses of his grace. We remember what he has done for us.

Lord, I remember what I was before I found you, and I give you
thanks for what I have become, by your grace.
I remember, Lord, and I thank you.

Clouded Vision

When your eyes are good, your whole body also is full of light.
But when they are bad, your body also is full of darkness.
—Luke 11:34

When Moses sent twelve men to spy out the Promised Land for Israel, ten came back with a bad report. When they saw the giants who occupied that land, they saw themselves as grasshoppers in comparison!

But two of the men, Joshua and Caleb, brought back a good report. They said, "We should go up and take possession of the land, for we can certainly do it. . . . The land . . . is exceedingly good" (Numbers 13:30; 14:7).

What gave the two groups of men such different perspectives? The ten terrified scouts had bad eyes—clouded vision. But Joshua and Caleb had eyes that were good—eyes of faith. They knew the Lord had promised them the land and led them to it. They said, "If the LORD is pleased with us, he will lead us into that land, . . . and will give it to us" (Numbers 14:8).

What's your perspective on your circumstances? Are things really as bad as you see them, or is your vision a little cloudy? Are your eyes flawed by the elements of unforgiveness, self-pity, fear, or pride? May God help us to clear our vision that we may truly number our blessings and claim his promises!

Lord, give me clear spiritual vision. May I view my difficulties with the eyes of faith and others' faults with the eyes of grace.

No Shadows There

*These are a shadow of the things that were to come; the reality,
however, is found in Christ.—Colossians 2:17*

*I*n the light of eternity, our present circumstances take
on new emphasis—or dissolve into nothingness. So many
things look different in God's light.

The shadows cast by the sun as it rises on a cloudless
morning are many times the length of the actual objects that
stand before the sun's rays. They are distorted images—much
larger than the objects they represent.

The Mosaic Law with its sacrifices, feasts, and celebrations
cast a long, early shadow of good things that were coming
for God's children. The old law could never make us truly
righteous in God's sight. It wasn't real; it was just a symbol
of what was real. All the lambs offered on the altar were only
symbols of the real Lamb who would die on a cross. As the
writer of Hebrews said, such rituals of Mosaic Law were
"only a shadow of the good things that are coming" (10:1).
The good thing that is coming is Christ.

How amazing to think that since we are spirit beings
confined to earthly bodies, we cannot yet contain the full
measure of God's glorious presence. The blessings we
have now as his beloved children are only shadows of the
unimaginable joy we will feel when we join him in paradise.

*Lord, keep the light of eternity shining on my life
so I may see things in the right perspective.
I look forward to a day when I see you face to face.*

A Chink in Every Hero's Armor

First take the plank out of your own eye.—Matthew 7:5

*N*ew believers often are disheartened when other Christians fall short of their expectations. Heroes are important, but when we see them as infallible, we're headed for trouble. As one after another falls off the pedestal we've put them on, we may even begin to believe we're the only ones staying true to God. That was the prophet Elijah's situation when he prayed for God to take his life. He saw the wickedness of his people, Israel, and believed he was the only servant of God left. (In reality, there were seven thousand others who had not bowed to Baal!)

When the weaknesses of a dear brother or sister are exposed, we must first ask God to remind us of our own imperfections. As we seek his grace for ourselves, we become more capable of understanding others' weaknesses. Next, we must lift up the fallen one into the Father's presence, see him or her in the light of God's love, and praise God for what we see.

Not only will these steps activate God's power in fellow Christians, they also will trigger a change in us. We will find ourselves reacting differently to those who have fallen, as we see their weaknesses—and our own—from God's perspective.

Lord, I free myself from the responsibility of trying to change anyone. Help me see others the way you see them through your eyes of mercy.

The Illuminated Word

*If they had [understood], they would not have crucified the
Lord of glory.—1 Corinthians 2:8*

It is often difficult to understand how those religious
leaders in Jesus's time, who had devoted their lives to
studying the Scriptures, could not recognize Jesus for who
he was. If anyone should have known the Messiah when they
encountered him, it was those men.

Their inability to accept Jesus as the Messiah is solid proof
that knowledge alone is not enough. When it comes to
spiritual things, there must be an enlightenment of the heart
before the Spirit of God's revelation begins to flow into it.
This order of doing things is something God takes pleasure
in. He loves to confound the wise and reveal the hidden
mysteries to the simple (see Matthew 11:25–26).

The sinful mind cannot accept God's leading. Paul said,
"It does not submit to God's law, nor can it do so" (Romans
8:7). But oh, what a transformation takes place when the
mind is renewed by the Holy Spirit and the Word of God!
In contrast to the sinful mind, which rejects the laws of the
Spirit, the renewed and enlightened mind embraces the
thoughts and purposes of God. Then, as if a big light bulb
has been switched on in the heart, the mind says, "Now I see.
Now I understand."

*Lord, I've missed out on so many things because of
my spiritual blindness. Illuminate my heart and mind
to see your truth for what it really is.*

Weekend Reflections

*I*n his book *The 7 Habits of Highly Effective People*, Stephen Covey tells how he received a new perspective on a subway ride one morning. His hopes for a quiet ride were dashed when a man and a couple of noisy children boarded the subway car. The children were loud, disturbing other passengers, yet the man to whom the kids belonged did nothing. With restrained exasperation, Stephen said to the man, "Sir, your children are disturbing a lot of people. I wonder if you couldn't control them a little more."

The man, lifting his eyes from a near daze, said, "Oh, you're right. I guess I should do something about it. We just came from the hospital where their mother died about an hour ago. I don't know what to think, and I guess they don't know how to handle it either."

Stephen immediately got a whole new perspective.

Ripples of Reflection

- Part of the evidence that we are walking in the Spirit comes when we see things from God's perspective. Consider a situation that is troubling you, and ask God to help you see it from his perspective.

- Think of three things God sees differently than you do. For example, he sees a person differently because, while we look on the outside, he sees the heart.

- How would your perspective change if you looked at everything you do as though you were measuring the results one hundred years from now?

When the Earth Trembled

The earth shook . . . ; Sinai itself was moved at the presence of God.—Psalm 68:8 NKJV

Imagine you are there, watching from a distance as, in one awe-filled moment, the Lord himself descends in fire upon Mount Sinai to meet Moses. Smoke billows up into the heavens, and the mountain trembles at the force of his presence. There is a long heavenly trumpet blast, and then, if you're still conscious, you hear the voice.

Thank God, we no longer come to a quaking Mount Sinai but to Mount Zion, the church covered by the blood of Christ (see Hebrews 12:18–22). Still, it is the knowledge of God's power displayed on Mount Sinai that moves us to "serve God acceptably with reverence and godly fear" (Hebrews 12:28 NKJV).

God help us when we find ourselves serving him with blasé and superficial worship! May God have mercy on us when we pray to him as though we were beseeching Santa Claus or the tooth fairy! Instead, we must worship him with reverence and awe, "for our God is a consuming fire" (Hebrews 12:29 NKJV).

Perhaps it is time we took a lesson from nature. If the earth knows to tremble at the presence of God, how much more should our hearts tremble when we come before him?

Oh God, my God, how awesome and mighty you are!
I love you, and yet I tremble at the thought
of One so great knowing and loving me.

New Isn't Necessarily Better

But we must be sure to obey the truth we have learned already.—Philippians 3:16 NLT

The kingdom of God is like a building constructed by God stone upon stone, revelation by revelation. But with all the great teachers we have had through history down to the present day, it's easy to get caught up in the excitement of discovery. While we should be thankful for revelations and grateful that God is speaking a fresh word to his people, we must not come to believe that the new revelation makes the old truth obsolete.

Even when new enlightenment and knowledge thrill and inspire us, the power is still where it has always been. As God reveals himself to us, the new revelation should point us, in some way, to the bedrock of our faith. The blood of the cross, the name of Jesus, the resurrection, his grace to us, and our faith in him—these are the things that must remain central. In embracing new methods of devotion, new ideas that inspire, we must not forget the tried-and-true power of prayer and study in the Word. "For no one can lay any foundation other than the one already laid, which is Jesus Christ" (1 Corinthians 3:11).

Father, you are the foundation of all that lasts.
Thanks for letting me share in what you are doing.
What I accomplish, I do by your strength.

Small Beginnings Plus God Equal Great Things

Who despises the day of small things?—Zechariah 4:10

When you decide to obey God, don't be surprised if your faith is immediately challenged. And don't be upset if you sometimes look foolish in others' eyes. Even some of your so-called friends may say, "Why are you doing that? Be reasonable! Don't you have any common sense?"

Sometimes reason and common sense can be our worst enemies, because common sense tells us to take the way of reason, while God tells us to take the way of faith. When God calls us to obey, we look to him to do what common sense says is impossible.

When Zerubbabel set out to build the temple, scoffers tried to discourage him and the other builders. They even "hired counselors to work against them" (Ezra 4:5). But God spoke through Zechariah and said, "Who despises the day of small things?"

Reason says, "What an insignificant thing to do!" God says, "Watch what I will do with your small things!" He will take your five loaves of bread and feed five thousand. Lead one soul to Christ, and God may use that one to touch the world. Don't look with shame on the day of small beginnings. If God is telling you to do it, rejoice, because God will complete it, and he will be glorified.

*Lord, forgive me for despising small beginnings,
for I know that it is in these small things that you are
glorified when the great results finally come.*

Are You Sure You Want Jesus to Come?

These are but the outer fringe of his works. . . . Who then can understand the thunder of his power?—Job 26:14

Often in church we pray something like, "Lord Jesus, come and dwell among us. Come in your power and grace, and touch your people." But sometimes I wonder, Do we understand what we are asking for?

Wherever Jesus went, there was both celebration and upheaval. Those who were delivered and healed rejoiced while others were annoyed. Isaiah prophesied concerning this, saying he would be a sanctuary for some, but for others he would be a rock that would cause men to fall (see Isaiah 8:14).

I'm convinced that many of us really don't want Jesus to show up in our churches. We want a god created in our image. A safe god. Someone who will only do things when we want him to and who will stay in his place the rest of the time. When we invite the Almighty God among us, he brings his own agenda; he doesn't follow ours. It's like inviting Billy Graham to speak at your conference but asking him not to make any reference to Jesus Christ. Good luck!

It could be dangerous to invite Jesus to your church. He may cause a disturbance. But one thing is for sure: if he comes, your church will never be the same again.

Lord, you are the Almighty God.
I resign myself to your agenda and your plan.
Send your glory and power, and give me the grace to receive it.

The Power of the Submitted Life

Submit yourselves therefore to God.—James 4:7 KJV

When I think of what it means to *submit*, I remember a family trip I took as a teenager. I had just received my driver's permit and insisted on driving every time an opportunity arose. We had rented a small motor home, and as we were making our way through Utah, my parents permitted me not only to drive but to read the map and choose the best route. I selected what appeared to be a shortcut. What I did not perceive from the map was that the "shortcut" was through a mountain pass. Suddenly I found myself driving the motor home over a small mountain road with dangerous turns. Eventually I had to stop and turn around because the road ahead was closed due to snow. By the time we reached the bottom of the mountain, my hands were shaking on the steering wheel, and I gladly submitted to my parents' expertise as drivers and navigators. What a relief it was to scoot out of the driver's seat and let Dad take charge again!

When we submit ourselves to God, we are saying, in effect, "Lord, you know the road ahead. You lead and I'll follow." It is an act of trust, a relinquishing of control. He knows the dangerous turns that lie ahead, and we need his expertise and direction.

*Father, I gladly turn over the wheel of my life to you.
I submit to your wisdom and your plan.
What power—and what relief—I feel as I do this!*

Weekend Reflections

*I*n *Teaching a Stone to Talk*, Annie Dillard says, "Churches are children playing on the floor with their chemistry sets, mixing up a batch of TNT to kill a Sunday morning. . . . Ushers should issue life preservers and signal flares; they should lash us to our pews. For the sleeping God may wake some day and take offense, or the waking God may draw us out to where we can never return."

Faith is more than believing in God for answered prayers. It is knowing God and understanding how great and awesome his mighty power is. If we perceive God to be little more than our grandfather in heaven who fulfills our every desire, how can we trust him with our lives, much less the universe?

Ripples of Reflection

- Why is an idol or graven image so detestable to God in relation to who he is?

- The Bible tells us that the earth trembles at the power of God (see Psalm 68:8). How does this relate to our understanding that we are loved and accepted by God because of the blood of Christ?

- When is the last time you stood amazed at the power of God? What were the circumstances?

- How can we truly love God and yet fear him? (see Acts 9:31; Proverbs 9:10)

Watch, Wait, and Listen!

In the morning I . . . watch and wait [for You to speak to my heart]. —Psalm 5:3 AMP

One of the most difficult things for us to do as Christians is to quietly wait and listen for God to speak to our hearts. So often it's easier for us to do and talk.

I once heard someone describe a hard-working Christian woman who found it difficult to wait on the Lord until someone told her that "to wait" actually meant "to serve." Now, she could do that!

Like that woman, many of us are looking for a different way of waiting than, well, just waiting. We are afflicted with the "Martha attitude," and too often we spend our time with the Lord—our prayer time—thinking more about what we are praying for instead of thinking about who we are praying to. Like Mary, we must learn to focus instead on the "one thing [that] is needed" (Luke 10:42), meditating on God's character, his grace, his beauty, seeking to know him as so much more than a source of blessing and provision.

Waiting means quietly listening. Learning to recognize his voice as it speaks to our hearts. Turning our thoughts from the things that need to be done to the One who fills the true need of our hearts.

Oh God, quiet my heart so that I can wait in your presence, learning your voice until my greatest quest as a Christian is to sit at your feet.

Speak, Lord!

*One thing I ask of the Lord. . . : that I may dwell in the house
of the LORD all the days of my life.*—Psalm 27:4

*W*hen I asked a relative what true love meant to him,
he said it's when two people can't stand being apart—not
necessarily side by side but at least in the same room. I think
he's right. Couples in love enjoy just being together, not
always talking but just being near each other. Sometimes a
husband and wife will settle into easy chairs and read separate
books or magazines "together."

We crave the same nearness when we're deeply in love
with the Lord. We don't always have to be praying to him
to show our love for him. And he doesn't have to always
be speaking to our hearts to show us he's there. Once, after
lifting up quite a long list of needs in prayer, I paused for a
moment and said quietly, "Speak, Lord," as I had so often
done before. Immediately I sensed the heart of my Father
saying, without my actually hearing the words, *Must I always
speak when you ask?*

That's when it occurred to me that perhaps God sometimes
wants us to simply be there with him with no grocery list
of requests, no agenda, no secret intentions. It's enough
just to be together. He wants not just our fellowship but a
relationship . . . not just communication but communion.

*Lord, teach me not to be impatient when I don't hear your voice.
Let me be happy just to sense your presence
and know that we are together.*

What Are You Listening For?

No one has heard, no ear has perceived, no eye has seen any
God besides you.—Isaiah 64:4

I am convinced that God shows himself more than we realize. Perhaps he speaks to us, but our hearts are not always tuned to the necessary wavelength. I am reminded of the story of the country dweller who visited his friend in New York City. As they walked down a busy street, there, amid all the busyness, the visitor remarked that he heard a cricket chirping. His city friend looked at him in disbelief and said surely it was impossible to hear a cricket above all the noise of the city. Walking over to a planter, the visitor reached down and pulled out the cricket. "Man hears what he listens for," he said.

God does not scream to make himself heard above the noise in today's busy lifestyles. Instead, he is there for those who turn off their natural ears and listen with their hearts for his still, small voice.

He spoke through Isaiah, saying, "When I called, no one answered, when I spoke, no one listened" (Isaiah 66:4). God "shows Himself active on behalf of him who [earnestly] waits for Him" (64:4 AMP). God is ready to reveal himself and to speak to those who will earnestly wait and listen.

Who are you waiting for? What are you listening for?

Lord, teach my heart to hear your voice,
to recognize it among the many voices I hear each day.
I rejoice in your work on my behalf.

He Who Has an Ear,
Let Him Hear

*He calls his own sheep by name. . . . His sheep follow him
because they know his voice.—John 10:3–4*

T am frustrated from time to time when an old friend
calls and puts me through the agony of guessing who he or
she is. If the caller is someone I haven't talked with in a long
time, I may not be able to link the voice with a face. On the
other hand, I quickly recognize the voices of those people I
speak with regularly. Usually, all they have to say is hello, and
in that instant I know who's calling.

The same is true when God speaks to us. If we're in touch
with him frequently, if we often sense him speaking to our
hearts, we know instantly that it is God's voice we hear.
But if we don't listen for it, if it's been a long time since we
were quiet enough to hear him speaking to us, we may not
recognize what's happening.

The only way we can quickly recognize God's voice is to
hear it often. In frequent times of communion with him, we
learn the sound of his voice, the warmth of his love, the
encouragement of his grace.

Then we wait, as Mary Magdalene waited at the tomb (see
John 20:10–16). And when, in that quietness, he calls our
names, we will instantly respond, "Rabboni!" We recognize
him as he calls to us because we have sat at his feet and heard
his voice time and time again.

*Lord, teach me to recognize your voice quickly. Be my shepherd,
Lord, and I will be one of your sheep who knows and responds
to what you say.*

A Sure Word

Samuel did not yet know the LORD: The word of the LORD had not yet been revealed to him.—1 Samuel 3:7

Oh, to hear a sure word from the Lord! We long to be like the prophet Samuel, who spoke the Word of the Lord with surety and boldness. The Bible says, "The LORD was with Samuel as he grew up, and he let none of his words fall to the ground" (1 Samuel 3:19). Everything Samuel declared came to pass. But Samuel's gift of prophecy didn't come until he learned to know God's voice. When God first spoke to him as a boy, Samuel did not recognize God's voice, but as he learned to listen and obey, he came to know and speak the sure word of God.

Do you recognize God speaking in your heart? If not, keep studying his Word and praying for his presence in your life. Then, when you know the sound of his voice, you can minister to others, speaking the voice of God in their lives. You will say something and find later that your words were exactly what God was saying.

Listen for God's voice, and be quick to obey in matters that at the time seem insignificant. Then God will entrust you with matters of greater importance. Over time, because of the character God has built in you, you will find joy in all his words and rejoice in their power to bring life.

Lord, I desire to know your voice and to bring a sure word at the right time so others will be called to hear and obey your voice as well.

Weekend Reflections

*W*hat does God's voice sound like? When the Father spoke from heaven when Jesus was baptized, apparently not everyone heard the same thing. Some said it thundered; some heard an angel (see John 12:28–29). Jesus heard his Father.

The fact remains: not everyone is listening when God speaks, and not everyone understands. Only those who know God will truly hear what he has to say. Seven times in Revelation 2–3, the Scriptures declare, "He who has an ear, let him hear what the Spirit says to the churches."

Ripples of Reflection

- Have you ever heard God's voice? What did it sound like?

- Spend some time examining Scripture references that describe when, where, and how God spoke. For example, in 1 Kings 19:12, God speaks in "a gentle whisper," but in Exodus 3:4 he calls to Moses from a burning bush.

- In your time alone with God, set aside a larger portion of time to be still and listen. Learn to recognize the voice of God speaking into your heart.

- How can we judge whether or not we are hearing the voice of God?

Stumbling over the Stumbling Stone

It is written: "See, I lay in Zion a stone that causes men to stumble."—Romans 9:33

You've probably seen those pictures that seem like one thing to some people and something else to others. One person looks at such a picture and sees an old lady while another sees a beautiful young miss. That's the way it was for the religious people of Jesus's day. They were anxiously awaiting the Messiah's appearing. But when he came, they didn't know him. They looked right at God and saw something else. Jesus said distress would befall them "because [they] did not recognize the time of [their] visitation from God" (Luke 19:44 NRSV). They were looking for God—and stumbled right over him.

Today we are capable of making the same mistake. In our quest for knowledge, discipline, and goodness, we can miss the whole point—fellowship with the One who makes us good. We search for him and think we have found him, only to later discover we have embraced counterfeit Christianity. Maybe you're searching for Jesus and looking too hard. He's a lot closer than you think. The apostle Paul said, "Men would seek him and perhaps reach out for him and find him, though he is not far from each one of us" (Acts 17:27).

Oh God, don't let me be one of those who misses the point. I want to see. I want to know the time of my visitation.

Hide and Seek

You will . . . find me when you seek me with all your heart.
—Jeremiah 29:13

Perhaps it's because God knows us so well, knows our love of seeking after things, that he sometimes seems to delight in being elusive. When we seek him, he often reveals himself to us one glory at a time. Slowly in our quest to know him, his character unfolds before us—and within us—like a stunning masterpiece that appears one brushstroke at a time.

Think of Elijah, who spent forty days and nights on Mount Horeb. Elijah probably looked for God in the wind that suddenly swirled and then in the earthquake that shook the mountain and in the fire that blazed down upon him. But God, perhaps delighting in being elusive, was not in any of the obvious places. Instead, Elijah finally found the Almighty God where he might have least expected him: in a still, small voice.

It would be so much easier today if we could find God in the obvious places: the booming thunder or the roaring surf or some other kind of natural phenomenon. Instead, he seems to show up in the most unexpected ways: as a babe in a manger . . . or as a stranger on the road to Emmaus. God knows we cherish a prize more dearly if we've struggled to find it. And he loves to be found.

Lord, I pray that you will open my eyes and sharpen my senses so I can see you in the everyday and in the unexpected.

Mountain Experiences

After leaving them, he went up on a mountainside to pray.
—Mark 6:46

The first time I stepped up to the edge of the Grand Canyon, the view literally took my breath away. In that moment I could sense nature gloriously bellowing out its song of praise to its Creator. It was an experience unlike anything I'd ever known.

I like to think that perhaps it was a similarly magnificent experience that explains, at least in part, why Jesus often went to the mountain. Maybe on the mountain he was able to clear his mind of the mundane and fix his eyes again on the eternal purpose at hand. The homes and villages that spread below him across the valley were amazing evidence of man's workmanship, but the mountain . . . ah, the mountain was familiar. This was *his* creation. His word had formed every peak and given life to every plant and creature that clung to the rocky soil. Perhaps on the mountain he prayed about another mountain—a hill, actually—he would later climb.

It was on that smaller mount that the Father would demonstrate his love for us again, fixing a point between heaven and earth where God could meet mankind without judgment. For there, justice was served, and mercy kissed that mount with each drop of blood.

Shepherd of my soul, I follow as you lead me up the mountain.
There, let me see things from your perspective
and pray the way you teach me.

To See Jesus

They came to Philip . . . , with a request. "Sir," they said, "we would like to see Jesus."—John 12:21

More than just a natural curiosity about the unknown, we should feel a hunger to see Jesus. But we will see him only as our natural passions fade. Our spiritual senses become focused only when the carnal is laid aside. So do not expect visions of glory to spring up in the middle of your physical surroundings. We must first "cast down" the temporal images before we can see the spiritual (see 2 Corinthians 10:5 KJV). As one fades from view, the other just naturally comes into focus.

As Helen Lemmel wrote so effectively, "Turn your eyes upon Jesus. Look full in His wonderful face. And the things of earth will grow strangely dim in the light of His glory and grace."

If we wish to see Jesus, we must deliberately and decisively turn away from idols, from selfish desires and ambition, from lazy and slothful devotion. As we turn away from these things of the world and turn, instead, toward our Lord and what is holy, we will begin to understand and know what was there all along but could not be discerned. The more we exercise our spiritual senses and put to death the carnal, the more enlightenment will be poured out on us.

Lord, may the real desire of my heart be to see your world, to turn my eyes to heavenly things, and to fix you as the goal of my affections.

Who Is Seeking Whom?

You will find him if you look for him with all your heart and with all your soul.—Deuteronomy 4:29

We must deliberately decide every day to seek the Lord. It's a decision we make for ourselves regardless of our circumstances. As Joshua said, "Choose for yourselves this day whom you will serve" (Joshua 24:15). Serving God must be a lifestyle, not just an emotional, one-time decision. Service demands "all your heart and all your soul" (Joshua 22:5). We're to seek him earnestly and call out to him, not with a halfhearted whimper, but with a plea for divine fellowship that arises from our innermost beings.

When I read the psalms of David, I become envious of such a friendship with God. But David did not find this close relationship through a once-a-week religious encounter. He daily encountered God. His desire was a constant thirst. We hear this heart-cry when he says, "As the deer pants for streams of water, so my soul pants for you, O God" (Psalm 42:1).

If you would know God's presence and sense his heart, cultivate your desire. Set out on your own search for God. Seek him, and you will find him just as they did, not far away but very close indeed.

Lord, replace this wandering heart of mine with a seeking heart that longs to know you, to hear your voice, to see your face.

Weekend Reflections

*A*n intimate relationship doesn't just happen. A great friendship is forged by communication, fellowship, and the fire of tough times. So it is with God. If we would really know him intimately, we must *pursue* knowing him. We must spend time with him—talking, listening, inviting him to walk with us through life's pleasure and pain.

Ripples of Reflection

- The psalmist wrote, "As the deer pants for streams of water, so my soul pants for you, O God" (Psalm 42:1). What similarities can be drawn between the thirsty deer and the man or woman who is in pursuit of knowing God?

- Think of three steps you can take now that will encourage you to pursue knowing God.

- Communication, fellowship, and walking together through tough times strengthen a relationship. Are any of these missing from your friendship with God? Are you weak in any of these areas? Which ones?

A Slave by Choice

So now offer [yourself] in slavery to righteousness leading to holiness.—Romans 6:19

*I*t seems to take us no effort at all to serve sin. But in reality we may have done many things to nurture that lifestyle. After all, it takes money, time, and other personal sacrifices to measure up to the world's standards and keep up with the pace of the party crowd. The more we expend ourselves on earthly pleasures, the more those pleasures demand of us . . . until they enslave us. Things that once brought pleasure soon become insatiable desires that gnaw away at us and are never fulfilled.

The key to living a victorious Christian life that resists this kind of bondage is to offer ourselves as servants of God. As we yield to God's righteousness and purity with the same energy and effort we once expended on fulfilling our selfish desires, we can become slaves to righteousness instead of slaves to wickedness.

Instead of a desire for something impure, the desire for God's presence can grow within us, becoming a thirst that is quenched only when we are in fellowship with him. This is the "slavery to righteousness leading to holiness."

Today, Lord, I willingly offer myself to you as an instrument of righteousness so that Christ may be formed and revealed in me.

I Am Not Who I Was

Unless a kernel of wheat falls to the ground and dies, it remains only a single seed.—John 12:24

The simple truth of being born again can be summed up like this: we die to who we are and rise from death to live as new creations through faith in the power of Jesus Christ. We are not reformed; we are reborn. We lose our old identities and find new ones in Christ Jesus.

The new creatures we become are nothing like our old selves. Our old natures were the seeds, the shells, that died in the ground so that our new creations could spring to life. Seeds do not have the same form as the plant; the acorn is not the oak tree. In the same way, we, as new creations in Christ, do not resemble our old natures. Our faith does not depend on what we brought to Christ, which really was nothing. All he wanted from us was our willingness to die to who we were. Now we "live by faith in the Son of God" (Galatians 2:20). "In Him we live and move and have our being" (Acts 17:28). We live not in the seed that was but as a new creation that exists by the resurrection power of Jesus Christ.

Don't be bound by who you were. That was the seed that died so the new creature could spring to life. You are a new person with a proud heritage and a rich inheritance!

Father, thank you that I am not who I was. You have made me a brand-new being. I have faith in your ability to cause me to live as a new creation.

Concern or Pride?

My heart is not proud, O LORD. . . . I have stilled and quieted my soul.—Psalm 131:1–2

The first time I read these verses, I was surprised to see the pairing of pride with worry. But how true it is: most worry is rooted in selfishness, self-centeredness, and pride. In contrast, unselfish people tend not to concern themselves with things they cannot change. They don't waste time worrying about what *might* happen.

When Jesus commissioned the apostle Peter, "Feed my sheep," he also indicated the kind of death Peter would have. Certainly, this was not an easy thing for Peter to swallow. He immediately pointed to John and asked, "Lord, what about him?" (see John 21:17–21).

Jesus's answer echoes down the ages to our ears today: "What is that to you? You must follow me" (John 21:22). Our responsibility is to follow him, letting God deal with others as he sees fit, leaving up to him those "great matters or things too wonderful" (Psalm 131:1).

To follow Jesus is to lay down our selfishness and pride and, in so doing, to relinquish our needless concerns and worries about things beyond our control. We're simply to deny ourselves—even denying ourselves self-indulgences such as worry—and take up the cross and follow him (see Matthew 16:24).

Lord, help me to give up my pointless anxiety and concern, laying all my cares on you, knowing how much you care for me.

Where Are You?

Then the LORD God called to Adam and said to him, "Where are you?"—Genesis 3:9 NKJV

When God asks a question, it isn't to gather facts. He already knows all the answers! God asks questions for our sake, not for his. It is the course God often chooses to bring us to a confession of truth. When God asks a question, it's time to 'fess up!

Where are you right now? Are you trying to hide from God, rejecting his love because you have too much pride to repent and admit your sinfulness? As Adam learned, when we run from the truth, we only deceive ourselves. There is no place to hide from God. And consider this: although God knew Adam and Eve were guilty, it was not in judgment that he pursued them. The first issue was love, then judgment. His first question of them was not, "What have you done?" but, "Adam, where are you?"

Adam ran. Love pursued.

Today God asks us the same question. Where are you? Are you trying to hide from his presence? What deed has brought you such shame that you would turn away from his love? Confess—and run to him.

I turn to you, Father. Where else can I go? "You alone have the words that give eternal life" (John 6:68 NLT).
I rejoice at the sound of your voice.

Reserved

They responded, "We will do everything the Lord has said; we will obey." —Exodus 24:7

*W*hat would happen if, in our churches on Sunday morning, everyone stood up and said wholeheartedly, "We will do everything the Lord has said; we will obey"? What power and glory could you know if you would declare the same? The truth is, this is exactly what God expects. He resists the proud but gives grace to the humble. And what greater humility is there than saying, "We will do everything you say, Lord"?

There are many who are ready to receive Jesus as their Savior. There are few who are willing to receive him as their Savior and Lord. But he will not be Savior unless he is also Lord. Often the people who are not living an abundant, overcoming life are the same ones who gasp, "Surely God does not want me to give up this!" Having this attitude is like hanging a sign on part of their heart that says, RESERVED FOR ME. As long as we are not fully obeying, we will not be fully blessed.

On the other hand, when we hear his voice and obey everything he says, God will not only be on our side, he will fight for us. As he told the Israelites, "I will be an enemy to your enemies and will oppose those who oppose you" (Exodus 23:22).

Jesus, what have you asked me to do that I have failed to obey? Show me the truth, Lord. I will do everything you say.

Weekend Reflections

*S*omeone once asked William Booth, founder of the Salvation Army, about the secret of his success. After several moments of quiet reflection, he said, "There have been men with greater brains or opportunities than I, but I made up my mind that God would have all of William Booth there was."

God is not looking for half-surrendered soldiers. He asks for full surrender.

Ripples of Reflection

- Is there something you know God is asking you to do that you have been resisting? What has been your excuse?

- Do you fear a full surrender to God? Why?

- The psalmist said, "I do not concern myself with great matters or things too wonderful for me" (Psalm 131:1). Surrender includes the relinquishing of needless concerns and worries of things beyond our control. What "great matters" do you need to surrender to God?

Why Did God Make Woman So Different?

"The two will become one flesh." . . . I am talking about Christ and the church.—Ephesians 5:31–32

God has compared marriage to his relationship with his church, so we can learn a lot about God as we look at the marriage relationship. For example, God created the woman in such a way that for her to be intimate, there must be relationship, which develops during the "getting to know each other" process. The relationship itself should be appreciated, not as merely a means to an end, such as sexual intimacy, but as something to be enjoyed for itself.

Through this we see how the heart of God desires a relationship with us, not merely the "I'll really love you, God, if you'll just answer my prayer" kind of association. In time we begin to enjoy the "getting to know you" journey. It becomes our passion, our real goal, more than just a means to receiving what God will do for us.

In marriage we see a symbol of God's undying commitment to us. God is in this for the long haul; he isn't interested in just short-term results. We commit to loving him, and he commits to loving us, even while we are changing and growing. This is the kind of love that must be in a marriage and in our relationship with God. Not "I'll love you when," but "I love you still."

Lord, I pray that I would have a strong resolve to find a deeper place of intimacy, a committed relationship, with you.

Mine, Yours, and His

If you cling to your life, you will lose it; but if you give it up for me, you will find it.—Matthew 10:39 NLT

We learn to say, "Mine!" early, and we struggle throughout our lives to give it up.

We may learn to share our possessions, but other things are not so easy to turn loose. Consider how we feel when our children interrupt our favorite TV shows, wanting to play with us; or when our sleep is interrupted by a call from the Holy Spirit to intercede for someone we barely know; or when our spouse gets sick and needs our help on our day off work.

Though we may not say the word out loud, our actions may shout, *Mine!* in situations such as these. The word itself does not have to be spoken for others to know how we feel. When our eyes are fixed so rigidly on our own needs, we fail to see their needs.

Cling, clutch, grip, and grab—and life will slide right through your fingers. But Jesus offers us the real recipe for abundant life: when we open our hands and our hearts and let go of those things we once clung to so selfishly, abundant life will come pouring in.

Father, everything I have is from you. But there are things I have clung to, thinking I own them. I lay them before you and consecrate them now.

True Love Is Vulnerable

Come to me quickly, for Demas . . . has deserted me. . . . Only Luke is with me.—2 Timothy 4:9–11

*P*aul wrestled with disappointment and loneliness when his other associates abandoned him and he was left with only Luke. But he also reaped a rich harvest from the seeds of love he had sown throughout the region.

Though everyone you love will not love you back, your love will not be wasted. Rest assured: there *will* be a harvest, and if you have sown your love generously, you will also reap generously (see 2 Corinthians 9:6). Sow anger; reap anger. Sow selfishness; reap isolation. Sow friendship; reap friends. No one ever said it better than C. S. Lewis in his book *The Four Loves*:

> To love at all is to be vulnerable. Love anything, and your heart will certainly be wrung and possibly be broken. If you want to make sure of keeping it intact, you must give your heart to no one, not even to an animal. Wrap it carefully round with hobbies and little luxuries; avoid all entanglements; lock it up safe in the casket or coffin of your selfishness. . . . The only place outside Heaven where you can be perfectly safe from all the dangers of love . . . is Hell.

God, you loved, and yet the world did not love you back. You give me the power to love others because I am loved by you.

Passion Makes a Difference

I am not ashamed, because I know whom I have believed.
—2 Timothy 1:12

*I*t is an accepted fact that only 30 percent of what we communicate is verbal. The rest of the message we're sending is carried by such unspoken things as our tone of voice and our body language. If we are going to be effective witnesses of the power of Jesus Christ, we must share the good news passionately. Others must not only hear the truth we're sharing but, by seeing the passion with which we carry the message, also understand how urgent this message is.

This passion arises from confidence. As the apostle Paul stated, "I am not ashamed, because I *know* whom I have believed" (emphasis added). It's not just that we know the facts. We know *him*. And that gives us the assurance to believe what he has said and done. Our relationship with him is the key to our passion.

We can know all the right things to say—have a great formula of sound theology—but if there is no passion, no confidence, or conviction in our words, we may have "lookers" but no "takers."

Lord, let the fervency of my relationship with you shine through the words I say so that others may believe you are alive in me.

Learning to Be Gentle

We were gentle among you, like a mother caring for her little children.—1 Thessalonians 2:7

Gentleness may be the most often forgotten attribute of Christ. No one was more focused and determined to complete his mission than Christ was, yet he knew how to be gentle when it was fitting. He was a "gentleman."

Gentleness is not always a convenient response, especially for some of us men. Often it seems so much easier to us to simply barge in, take control, demand attention, and complete whatever action is needed. Occasionally that kind of response is appropriate. But often an attitude of gentleness is much more beneficial and nurturing to all concerned.

Gentleness can be a natural response because it is a fruit of the Spirit. As we allow the Spirit to work within us, it will bear fruit, and gentleness will flow from us just as naturally as joy. Consider how much easier it is to hear truth wrapped in the fragrance of gentleness rather than having it blasted at us in a harsh and arrogant way. Love, too, goes a lot further when it's steeped in gentleness rather than soaked with demands.

To become more Christlike, we must become more like the one who said, "I am gentle and humble in heart" (Matthew 11:29).

Lord, you are the perfect combination of gentleness and strength; in you I find the power to be gentle myself.

Weekend Reflections

*L*ove should not be something we keep but something that we give away. As Jesus said to Peter, "Do you love me? . . . Feed my sheep" (John 21:17). Mother Teresa said it like this: "Love, to be real, must cost. It must hurt. It must empty us of self" (*USA Today,* November 17, 1986).

Ripples of Reflection

- What three things about your spouse or your closest friend are you *most* thankful for?

- Love includes risk and vulnerability. When was the last time you were really transparent with someone?

- Selfishness kills love. What three unselfish things will you do this week for someone you love?

Was He an Angel?

"Lord, when did we see You . . . , and did not minister to You?"—Matthew 25:44 NKJV

It was nine o'clock. I had just finished rehearsal, and I was exhausted, hungry, and ready to go home. Just as I reached for the light switch, a man stepped through the door. He walked to the front of the meeting room, saw the piano, and asked if he could play.

The man was untidy and was wearing several layers of clothes, all rumpled and soiled. I reluctantly told him he could play. But after several minutes of listening to songs I didn't recognize, I told him I needed to go home. He said, "Sure," and quit playing. I asked him his name, but he answered, "Oh, I'm nobody."

When I insisted he *was* somebody, he said, "Look, I know what you're trying to do. Don't bother." We walked out, and I locked the door and said good-bye. Later it occurred to me, *What if he was an angel?*

Suddenly I wanted to go back and find him, hoping we could talk some more. Then it hit me: I had been eager to serve the man if he was an angel. But if he was just another vagrant looking for a handout, I was too tired. I felt ashamed, remembering Jesus's words: "Whatever you did not do for one of the least of these, you did not do for me" (Matthew 25:45).

Father, forgive me for turning away from serving
"the least of these." Let me love them with your compassion
and bless them as you bless me.

43

Good Impressions

We were not looking for praise from men, not from you or anyone else.—1 Thessalonians 2:6

The goal of ministry service must be to point others to Jesus, not to ourselves. Our aim is not to impress them with our abilities, to have them think, *My, isn't he eloquent!* The sign of effective ministry is when others exclaim, "My, isn't Jesus wonderful!"

This means that as we minister, we lay down our desire for affirmation, our need for praise and applause. We will be effective ministers when people walk away feeling impressed with Jesus more than with our own gifts and abilities.

Jesus told us, "Anyone who does not take his cross and follow me is not worthy of me. Whoever finds his life will lose it, and whoever loses his life for my sake will find it" (Matthew 10:38–39). In our total commitment to him, we lose our life for his sake. And we choose not to glory in our sacrifice but in his. As one dear sister of the faith said, "You think you're livin' now? Honey, you ain't lived 'til you been livin' for Jesus!"

We preach the gospel of Christ, not our gospel. We lift up his cross, his life, his greatness, and lay down our own. And in doing so, we find new and abundant life.

Father, I pray that through me your light will shine. May they see your life in me as I lose myself in you.

What's in It for Me?

*Love one another. As I have loved you, so you must love
one another.—John 13:34*

When folks are "too nice," we often suspect they have
ulterior motives. It seems rare to find people who bestow
kindness when they have nothing to gain.

Truly unselfish love can only come from God. This is the
kind of love described in those familiar verses in the Gospel
of John: "For God so loved the world, that he gave his only
begotten Son" (3:16 KJV), and, "Greater love hath no man
than this, that a man lay down his life for his friends" (15:13
KJV).

Sometimes the way we take advantage of God's selfless love
seems blatantly shameful. Too often when we come before
God's presence, our first tendency is to pull out our wish
list: "God, since I know I have your attention . . ." Instead of
asking only for selfish benefits, we need to ask God to give
us hearts filled with a passion for communion with him. We
need to thank him for the unequaled love he shows us—and
ask him to help us show that same love to others.

May God grant us the grace to seek him for the sake of
selfless, unpretentious love. There is no other way we can do
it, for he is the only source of such unselfish love.

> *Father, there is no fountain of life besides you.*
> *When I love, let it be with the love of Christ.*
> *When I hate, let it be only what you hate.*

Loving Jesus

Again Jesus said, "Simon son of John, do you truly love me?
. . . Take care of my sheep."—John 21:16

Jesus's instructions to us to serve one another do not go over too well in a society that lives by the rule "Look out for number one." But those who know God also know that the one who is serving is the one who truly receives. We learn this lesson by following his example. We also learn it because sometimes he places us in positions where we have no other options!

We show our love for Christ by serving others, and our attitudes as we serve them show how genuine our love for him really is. If our attitude is *What a chore!* we are showing that our love for Christ may not be as deep as we would like to think it is.

We find joy in service by picturing ourselves serving Christ. For example, instead of seeing ourselves helping a whining child or comforting a helpless invalid, we see ourselves serving Christ. This is where true freedom to serve becomes possible. We do it as though we are "working for the Lord, not for men" (Colossians 3:23).

"Take care of my sheep," Jesus tells us.

"Lord, you know that I love you," we reply.

"Take care of my sheep," he echoes.

And then he guides us toward the pasture.

Lord, give me eyes to see those around me in the light of your love. Instead of seeing their faces, may I see yours.

The Motivational Factor

Though I bestow all my goods to feed the poor, . . . but have not love, it profits me nothing.—1 Corinthians 13:3 NKJV

What motivates you in the work you do for Christ? Why do you do what you do? Is it out of a sense of obligation? Do you believe it is required of you because you are a child of God? Or is it from your drive to succeed, to be somebody?

The apostle Paul said that even if we give everything we have to the poor, and even if we give our bodies "to be burned," it profits nothing if we don't have love.

"Nothing?" we ask. "You mean all those times I gave to the local mission and worked in the nursery at church amount to nothing just because I don't have love?"

That's right. Nothing. Absolutely nothing.

In Jesus's life and words we see the only real reason for service: "I am come that they might have life," he said (John 10:10 KJV). His whole mission was accomplished because God so loved us.

True love gives. The only work, the only sacrifice acceptable to God is the one given out of love. Any other is tainted with the smell of self-service; and love, the Bible teaches us, "is not self-seeking" (1 Corinthians 13:5).

Father, you are the source of the love I share with others.
I look to you to fill me with your pure love
so that I may love what you love.

Weekend Reflections

The true foundation for serving others is seeing the face of Christ in those we serve, no longer seeing them as ordinary people but as eternal spirits who will spend forever somewhere. It was C. S. Lewis who said in *The Weight of Glory*, "You have never talked to a mere mortal . . . but it is immortals that we joke with, work with, marry, snub and exploit—immortal horrors or everlasting [splendours]."

Ripples of Reflection

- Jesus revealed service as the path to greatness. Think of some great people who practiced this kind of greatness.

- What are *you* doing to serve Christ by serving others?

- Have you served "angels unawares"? (Hebrews 13:2 KJV). When? How does it compare with ministering to "the least"? (Matthew 25:40).

All of Me

*O LORD, you have searched me and you know me. . . . You
are familiar with all my ways.—Psalm 139:1–3*

An old adage defines a friend as "one who knows all about you—and likes you anyway." Few of us are secure enough to let our real selves show, except to those friends and relatives who are closest to us. We become actors, learning at an early age to portray a different, more polished, role in public.

We may become so accustomed to this acting that we don't even realize we're doing it. Yet God knows. He knows every part of us, every secret role we play, every hidden thing we do. He has given us diverse traits and characteristics so that we can be the people he wants us to be. He's perfectly familiar with that part of us we consider too playful and immature or too brassy and dramatic—the part that, when it shows, causes us to shudder and hope no one notices. But God sees. And he loves us anyway.

What freedom we find when we realize we can stand before our Creator without dread, knowing he sees every intimate part of us and yet does not despise those traits that we consider less than desirable. God knows all our ways, because he wove together all our parts (see Psalm 139:13).

*Lord, I acknowledge that you created me,
and I thank you for all that I am, even for the parts of me
that sometimes seem so undesirable.*

The Way to Defeat a Bully

Then you will know the truth, and the truth will set you free.
—John 8:32

In third grade I landed in a new school in a new city and had not yet made many new friends, but I had crossed paths with a bully named Eddie. He was a pest in every sense of the word.

He was always punching me—never really hurting me but hitting just hard enough to annoy me. I tried to avoid him, but it seemed he always knew where to find me. I can't remember the day the conflict finally ended, but eventually we came to respect each other.

The enemy of our souls is much like Eddie. He always knows where we are, and his most common weapons are annoying nuisances more than anything else. He uses deception, condemnation, boasting, and other practices that usually don't really hurt us immediately as much as they knock us around and seek to wear us down.

If you keep running into condemnation in your life, you can know assuredly that it is either from Satan or from your own soul. God's weapons—such things as truth and love—are not like Satan's at all.

Do you want to defeat the bully of your soul? "Stand firm then, [wearing] the belt of truth . . . , [and] the breastplate of righteousness" (Ephesians 6:14).

Lord, your truth sets me free.
I'm so glad you don't use condemnation to change me.
Instead, you speak the truth in love and make me free.

Words of Life

Reckless words pierce like a sword, but the tongue of the wise brings healing.—Proverbs 12:18

Words said with little or no thought can pierce our heart like a sword. But when we are the target of such words, we can choose how we respond: we can receive them as lies, or we can hold to what God has already declared.

The biblical account of Gideon has him "threshing wheat in a winepress to keep it from the Midianites" (Judges 6:11). Then an angel of the Lord came and sat down under a nearby oak tree. He said, "The LORD is with you, mighty warrior" (verse 12). Though Gideon felt like a cowering and defeated man, God spoke words of life to him, and Gideon chose to believe what God said in spite of his feelings and the evil report of the day.

Friend, we must choose to believe what God says rather than believing the harsh words others may level against us. The apostle Paul wrote, "Let God be true, and every man a liar" (Romans 3:4). God cannot lie. What he says is true, and he has said we have worth (see Matthew 10:29, 31); we belong to him (see 1 Peter 2:9); and we are called children of God (see 1 John 3:1).

Do not let others' critical remarks cause you to forget your heritage. You are a child of God—created, chosen, and cherished.

Lord, I turn to you. You alone have "the words of eternal life" (John 6:68).

Have You Heard What God Says about You?

Fear not, for I have redeemed you; I have summoned you by name; you are mine.—Isaiah 43:1

I listened as a young man told me, "All my life they predicted I would never amount to anything," he said. "I finally believed them."

Our world is full of people who are held captive by the lies of others. Perhaps they heard, "Can't you do anything right?" Or, "Face the facts. You don't have what it takes."

Some strong-hearted people are able to throw off this kind of negative feedback, but in others the wounds are buried so deep that the person may not even recall them at a conscious level. But the message isn't forgotten.

As we open our hearts to the Father's tender mercy, his healing love does radical things to us. It closes the wounds cut by those harsh words so long ago, and we find our true reason for existence, our purpose for living. Best of all, we begin to experience real joy within.

Regardless of how many lies we have listened to and believed, we need to know what God has to say about us: that we are treasures in his eyes and that we cannot even count the times he thinks of us! We must choose now to believe what God says about us rather than to believe other people's lies—and even our own.

Jesus, I will come to you and listen for the truth, and I will renounce and reject the lies the world tries to make me believe.

Something Out of Nothing

God . . . chose those who are powerless to shame those who are powerful.—1 Corinthians 1:27 NLT

God seems to delight in calling people who think they aren't qualified. His reason is clear: he doesn't want us depending on our own resources but on his.

When God called Moses to be Israel's deliverer, Moses's reply was, "O Lord, please send someone else to do it" (Exodus 4:13). God told Gideon to send most of his army home so the Israelites would not boast that their own strength had saved them from the Midianites (see Judges 7:2). The three hundred men who remained were a greater force with God on their side than the original thirty-two thousand without God.

God definitely uses our abilities, but he receives the greatest glory from those who may not possess great talent but are available and compliant to his will. The greatest leaders are always those who stay in touch with their own frailty. They know their weaknesses and depend on God to make up the difference.

God knows we aren't perfect. He is very much aware that we are human and will make mistakes. Still, he chooses us and declares us righteous. He takes the mediocre and makes them fantastic. He uses the meek and gives them the inheritance. That's our God!

Lord, I will depend on your heavenly, supernatural resources to empower me to do what I cannot do aside from you.

Weekend Reflections

Self-acceptance begins with knowing we are loved by God. If God accepts us, we can accept ourselves. This self that we accept, of course, is the self we find in Christ. As C. S. Lewis said, "The very first step is to try to forget about the self altogether. Your real, new self . . . will not come as you are looking for it. It will come when you are looking for him" (*Mere Christianity*).

Ripples of Reflection

- How can your unique qualities serve the body of Christ?

- What are some visible changes you see in your new self that are totally different from your old self?

- Lay out before God what you dislike about yourself. What does he have to say about your opinion?

The Blesser or the Blessed?

It is more blessed to give than to receive.—Acts 20:35

For many of us, humility may be the most elusive of Christ's attributes. Once we think we have achieved it, the ugly head of pride suddenly pops up, and we realize just how far away from humility we really are.

When I was greeting churchgoers after services one Sunday, a particularly large, unkempt, older lady asked if she could have a hug. I obliged and she happily wrapped her dimpled arms around me and squeezed. I also received a wet kiss on the cheek. Afterward I was feeling sort of lofty about my willingness to be a blessing to this overly sweet, rather childish misfit when a quiet voice within me said, *Who was blessed, you or her?*

In my heart I knew the truth. Jesus told his disciples, "He who is least among you all—he is the greatest" (Luke 9:48).

That's what I sensed him reminding me that day after church: when you accept a heartfelt hug and an enthusiastic kiss from an overweight, disheveled champion of the faith, you're receiving it from me.

Yes, I was the one who was blessed that day. As she planted her wet lips against my cheek, it was Christ's kiss I received. She was the blesser, and I was the blessed.

Lord, please forgive me for the times you have blessed me through others and I haven't noticed.

Pride Unmasked

A man's pride brings him low, but a man of lowly spirit gains honor.—Proverbs 29:23

As Christians we're taught the godliness of self-sacrifice. But some of us have a tendency to glory in that sacrifice, to call attention to our noble deeds. Our challenge, then, is to serve humbly and quietly, to find joy in the service itself, and to work in areas that do not directly improve our image or our reputation.

We must always be mindful of our need to serve God in all we do. And we must understand that it is God who prompts us to serve in the first place and who gives us hearts that can love unselfishly. By serving others, we carry the love of God to others—the love we have first experienced ourselves.

Self-sacrificing service with no thought of receiving something in return puts God's love into action. It is birthed from divine compassion and comes straight from the heart of Christ, the one who looked on the multitudes with compassion and saw them as helpless "sheep without a shepherd" (Matthew 9:36). To save them—and us—he became the Good Shepherd, laying down his life for his hurting little lambs. That compassion, completely lacking pride, is our example.

Lord, no sacrifice I can make can compare to yours.
I will resist the tendency to glory in service
and instead choose to serve for your glory.

Do This, and the Devil Will Run!

God opposes the proud, but gives grace to the humble.
—James 4:6

*M*any of us have quoted this verse to those struggling with temptation: "Resist the devil and he will flee from you" (James 4:7 KJV). But we often forget the first part of the verse: "Therefore submit to God."

Do you want the grace (favor) of God to be upon you? Submission is the key. Pride says, "I can do this." Submission says, "I can do all things through Christ" (Philippians 4:13 NKJV).

The apostle James wrote, "Humble yourselves in the sight of the Lord, and he shall lift you up" (4:10 KJV). We have a choice to make. God can allow us to fall flat on our faces so that we become humble and submitted, or we can humble ourselves. I don't know about you, but I choose the latter.

And notice that James said we're to humble ourselves "in the sight of the Lord." If we publicly humble ourselves, we may feel tempted to glory in it—to feel proud of our humility, thinking, *Look at me. I'm sacrificing for the Lord.* But when we humble ourselves in places nobody sees, there is less temptation for pride. This is the kind of humility that God honors and rewards. Public humility may bring the praise of men, but private humility will bring the public grace and favor of God.

Holy Lord, I submit to you—
to your authority, to your lordship, to your power.
Please forgive me for my pride and arrogance.

The Key Ingredient of Greatness

Let him that thinketh he standeth take heed lest he fall.
—1 Corinthians 10:12 KJV

The truly great are not impressed with themselves. They don't sit around thinking about their "standing." They are in touch with their humanity and aware of how temporary life really is.

When I think of greatness, one man who always comes to mind is Billy Graham. I once saw an interview where he was posed the question, "When you get to heaven, is there any major question you would like to ask God?"

He quickly replied, "Yes. I want to ask the Lord why he chose me."

The truly great are very confident, but their attitude is not so much self-confidence as it is God-confidence. It is the expectancy and hope that springs from knowing that whose we are is more important than who we are.

What is the key ingredient to greatness? What do great men and women strive for? They don't work for greatness. No, they humble themselves in obedience—and in doing so, find greatness. Their example is the greatest man who ever lived, one who did not aim for prestige but "made himself nothing" (Philippians 2:7). Then God exalted him from "nothing" to the peak of greatness.

Lord Jesus, save me from the trap
of pride and the deceitfulness of self-promotion.
Without you I can do nothing, but with you I can do all things.

Who Me, God?

. . . so that your faith might not rest on men's wisdom, but on
God's power.—1 Corinthians 2:5

D o you feel inadequate? Congratulations! You've met the first requirement for becoming an instrument of God!

God rarely chooses the most competent persons to do his work. Consider the perceived inadequacies of these Bible heroes: Abraham thought he was too old, Moses thought he couldn't speak well enough, Saul was from the wrong family, Gideon was too weak, and David was too young. In each case God capitalized on their insufficiency and did what appeared to be impossible. Abraham fathered a child, Moses led a nation, Saul became king, Gideon became a war hero, and David brought down the local bully!

I love that about God, don't you? So often he passes right by the champion standing in the spotlight and chooses, instead, the One Most Unlikely to Succeed as his chosen representative.

What's your excuse? Maybe it's "But I've never done that before," or, "I didn't go to college." Isn't it funny how we sometimes argue with God, listing our inadequacies, even though he is well aware of our every deficiency. Still, he chooses us and says, "My grace is sufficient for you, for my power is made perfect in weakness" (2 Corinthians 12:9).

Lord, in the strength of your Spirit, I will move out to
accomplish what you've set before me (see Zechariah 4:6).

Weekend Reflections

God says the way to greatness is service. The road to the top requires us to humble ourselves "before the Lord" (James 4:10). C. S. Lewis spoke of this humility when he said, "The Eternal Being, who knows everything and who created the whole universe, became not only a man but (before that) a baby, and before that a fetus inside a woman's body. If you want to get the hang of it, think how you would like to become a slug or a crab" (C. S. Lewis, quoted in Bruce Demarest, *Jesus Christ: The God-Man*).

Ripples of Reflection

- Many successful businesses have discovered the principle that service leads to greatness. Why do you think service has brought about their success?

- Think of famous figures who began to "believe their own press" and soon met with destruction (see Proverbs 16:18).

- Why does humility come before honor? (see Proverbs 18:12). Identify some examples of this truth.

The Mysterious Ways of the Lord

*When he had spit on the man's eyes and put his hands on him,
Jesus asked, "Do you see anything?"—Mark 8:23*

There are many accounts of Jesus healing the sick. In most
instances he simply touched them and they were healed. In
his compassion he reached out to the masses, touching the
untouchable, loving the unlovely.

But in the case of the blind man at Bethsaida, Jesus spat
on the man's eyes. He spat on the man! Why would he
choose to heal someone in such an unusual, even shocking,
way? Perhaps it's because God refuses to be boxed in by
our boundaries. Just when we think we have everything
all figured out, he changes the methodology. Such puzzles
caused David to cry out, "Show me your ways, O LORD,
teach me your paths" (Psalm 25:4).

I believe these glimpses into the divine ways of God are
invitations. They appeal to us to study and meditate on the
amazing and inspiring life of Christ and to enter the higher
realms of relationship with him where we may discover his
purposes and plans for our own lives. Yes, and even gain
greater understanding. Not every why and how will be
answered, but the more we know him, the more we trust
him. The greater our confidence in his awesome ability and
mysterious design, the more our souls are at rest.

*Lord, teach me your ways.
Lift me up to that higher plane so that I can hear your voice
and get a glimpse of the heavenly design.*

The Thoughts of the Lord

As the heavens are higher than the earth, so are . . . my thoughts than your thoughts.—Isaiah 55:9

*H*ave you ever looked at the heavens and wondered, *God, what are you doing?* It boggles the human mind to contemplate the workings of Holy God. In fact, there are not many things of the spiritual realm that make much sense to the natural mind. That is why we must set our minds above carnal, human reasoning. As Paul wrote, "Those who live according to the sinful nature have their minds set on what that nature desires; but those who live in accordance with the Spirit have their minds set on what the Spirit desires" (Romans 8:5).

To set our minds on spiritual things, we must abandon our old thought systems, because the old ways of thinking don't work in a spiritual kingdom. We're instructed, "Let the wicked forsake his way and the evil man his thoughts" (Isaiah 55:7).

There will always be those who feel compelled to reason everything out, as if there must be a logical explanation. But some things simply cannot be sorted out with natural reasoning. Although our thoughts can be lifted into another, heavenly realm, we still will not understand all of God's workings. What we can know is that God is working in our lives. We can believe that.

Almighty God, as I lift my mind to you now, your thoughts begin to consume my thoughts, and I find peace.

To Be Continued

God has chosen to make known among the Gentiles the glorious riches of this mystery.—Colossians 1:27

Everyone loves a good mystery. There's just something about having only a part of the answer that rattles our curiosity and makes us eager to know the rest of the story. Perhaps there's a bit of the detective in all of us that wants to see if our suspicions are accurate.

Before Jesus ascended to the Father, his disciples tried to solve the mystery he had introduced them to. "Is now the time you will restore the kingdom to Israel?" they asked.

"It is not for you to know what only my Father knows," Jesus replied (Acts 1:6–7, my paraphrase).

Today we, too, ask questions that God will not answer yet. Jesus meant what he said; some things are not for us to know. Instead of trying to discern what God has said is indiscernible, we should focus on the mystery of knowing Jesus Christ more intimately.

There is so much about him to explore, yet we can only know part of the story until we join him in heaven. As Paul wrote, "Now we see but a poor reflection as in a mirror; then we shall see face to face. Now I know in part; then I shall know fully" (1 Corinthians 13:12). The story is ever unfolding . . . to be continued.

Oh the mystery of your grace, my Lord.
Breathe on the sparks of my heart so that they will blaze
with a passion to see your glory.

The Wonder of It All

The wisdom of the wise will perish, the intelligence of the
intelligent will vanish.—Isaiah 29:14

In an acronym for worship, I think the *w* should stand for *wonder*, for how can we truly worship God without a sense of wonder? He is so much greater than our knowledge of him, and that greatness causes us to wonder about the part we do not know. Wonder also explains why worship cannot be confined to quiet moments in cathedrals. Worship happens when we stand beneath a clear Montana sky and wonder at the artistry that created such a backdrop. It happens when we listen to the surf crashing against a California coast or hear the trills of a canary or gaze at the tiny fingers of a newborn baby. Pondering such things moves us toward worship.

Some have called Christmas the season of wonder because it's a time when we wonder how God became a baby crying in a stable, how heaven orchestrated an angelic concert for a handful of shepherds, and how a place such as little Bethlehem was chosen for Jesus to make his entrance. Considering this, it should not surprise us that the prophet Isaiah said, "His name shall be called Wonderful" (Isaiah 9:6 KJV), meaning literally "full of wonder."

Creator of all things, your name is Wonderful,
and I am full of wonder when I consider who you are,
and I stand amazed at your majesty.

A Kingdom of Fools

God hath chosen the foolish things of the world to confound the wise.—1 Corinthians 1:27 KJV

No wonder nonbelievers think we are fools—we who were common, destined to lives without notoriety, now claiming to be loved by a king who declared us so valuable that he offered his life in exchange for our freedom. This king promised that if we would believe in him, he would receive us into a kingdom not of this world—a kingdom where the simple reign as princes and priests alongside him, where unimaginable wealth is so commonplace that the streets are paved with gold and the rarest of jewels are so plentiful that they're used as construction material.

No wonder they think us fools when we claim that not only does he know our names, but he hears our silent prayers as well and knows when we rise and when we sleep. No wonder they scoff when we say he let the convicted go free by paying the ransom of the guilty, the shamed, and debased. No wonder they laugh when we say he has been seen washing the feet of ordinary peasants, much as a servant would.

Who would believe such a fairy tale? Who would call such a king a king at all?

"Where could such a kingdom be?" they say.

"Ah," we answer, "it's closer than you think. In fact, 'the kingdom of heaven is at hand'" (Matthew 3:2 KJV).

Almighty God, what a wonder you are! You have dumbfounded the sages and philosophers with the simple things.

Weekend Reflections

*S*ome things are not meant for us to know. The wonder of such "unknowables" reminds us why he is the Almighty God and we are the created ones. In A.D. 399, Saint Augustine said, "People travel to wonder at the height of mountains, at the huge waves of the sea, at the long courses of the rivers, at the vast compass of the ocean, at the circular motion of the stars—and they pass by themselves without wondering" (quoted by Dr. Paul Brand and Philip Yancey in *Fearfully and Wonderfully Made*). There is always a reason for wonder.

Ripples of Reflection

- What questions are you wrestling with in your heart right now?

- What are some possible reasons why you perceive no immediate answers?

- Set aside a time of wonder in your worship time, thinking about some of the amazing aspects of God.

Golden Bowls

They were holding golden bowls full of incense, which are the
prayers of the saints.—Revelation 5:8

Most believers have experienced times when their prayers seem about as powerful as a defective bottle rocket. They seem to rise up about ten feet and fizzle. When these experiences happen repeatedly, we begin to think, *I might as well not pray today; my prayers seem so empty.*

When God doesn't respond to our prayers immediately or in the way we want, it doesn't mean he isn't listening or that he isn't aware of our situation.

God sees our tears. His ears are attentive to our cries, as David said (see Psalm 34:15). He sees our faithful obedience, even when the anointing is not there and the heavens seem plated with brass. Consider the biblical character Cornelius, a "God-fearing" centurion but a man who had not experienced faith in Jesus Christ and knew nothing of the power of the Holy Spirit. Yet one day an angel of God appeared to him and declared, "Your prayers and gifts to the poor have come up as a memorial offering before God" (Acts 10:4).

Our prayers are precious to God. He sees all that we do and hears every word we speak to others and to him. Take courage and remain faithful. Your prayers are lifted up to him in "golden bowls."

Lord, thank you for always hearing my prayers.
Help me to remember your promises
and remain obedient in moments of doubt and uncertainty.

Honest to God

The LORD is near to all who call upon Him, . . . who call upon Him sincerely and in truth.—Psalm 145:18 AMP

When we pray, there is one thing God is certainly looking for: honesty. Are we praying the truth? Are the words we speak sincere, arising from an earnest heart?

Jesus rebuked the Pharisees for hypocrisy in their prayers, and today he commands us, "Do not keep on babbling like pagans, for they think they will be heard because of their many words" (Matthew 6:7). Our Lord is not concerned with whether we are packing every moment of our prayer time with constant speaking. Rather, he is looking for an honest heart that will pour out before him its innermost thoughts and desires.

God wishes to listen to, to commune with, us in our sincerity. He wants to hear from the real us, not some religious character we have created because we're afraid to be honest with God and let him see who we really are.

So when we pray, we open ourselves and pour out our hearts to the Father genuinely and totally. In doing so, we obey Jesus's words: "When you pray, do not be like the hypocrites" (Matthew 6:5). We joyfully come to him in honesty.

Lord, I want to be honest with you. Holy Spirit, walk with me through the corridors of my heart and examine it with me.

Say It with Your Mouth, Not Just Your Heart

If anyone says to this mountain, "Go, throw yourself into the sea," and . . . believes . . . , it will be done for him.
—*Mark 11:23*

*M*any people, especially men, have a hard time expressing their feelings—sometimes because they don't want others to know what they're feeling and thinking and other times because they think it should be obvious to others what they think and feel. (And God forbid they should waste time expressing the obvious!) How many times have you made the mistake of not speaking up because you wrongly assumed your friends or family members already knew how you felt?

Just as we should express our feelings, we should also speak out about what we believe. It isn't enough to believe silently in our hearts and never express what we know to be the truth. Consider the confessions of those who were strong in faith. Before Abraham saw the sacrificial animal to be substituted for his son, he proclaimed, "God will provide himself a lamb" (Genesis 22:8 KJV). And the little boy David believed so completely in his God that before he threw the first stone at Goliath, he said, "This day the LORD will hand you over to me" (1 Samuel 17:46).

Yes, God knows what we believe in our hearts, but he wants us to say it as well as believe it. Say what you believe, and believe what you say. That is the kingdom principle.

Lord, I say what I believe: "You are Lord of all." Open my eyes to see the power in what I say and to think before I speak.

69

He Spent the Night in Prayer

He went out to the mountain to pray, and continued all night in prayer to God.—Luke 6:12 NKJV

*S*ometimes people who must make pivotal decisions with long-range implications spend days asking what their friends think or consulting with the "experts" or seeking advice from self-help gurus—and less than five minutes seeking God's will about the issue at hand.

But before Jesus chose his twelve apostles, he spent the night in conversation with his Father. Even though he was the Son of God, he did not feel it a waste to spend the whole night in prayer. By his example he taught us that major decisions require major prayer and that one of the best ways to use our time is in communion with God.

Psalm 1:1 tells us, "Blessed is the man who walks not in the counsel of the ungodly" (NKJV). We cannot have peace or wisdom regarding our circumstances when we spend our time seeking the advice of "the ungodly." And who are the ungodly? Those whose minds are not in the process of being transformed (see Romans 12:2).

Jesus sought the wisdom of the Father. He spent the night in prayer when he chose his board of directors. What about you? Do you pray when you hire or fire someone? When you change jobs, careers, or locations, do you seek your Father's counsel? Do you have other important decisions that would benefit from godly wisdom? (Are there any other kinds of decisions?)

Jesus, "order my steps in thy word" (Psalm 119:133 KJV). What is your word concerning my life and the decisions I must make?

Sweating It Out

*Being in agony, he prayed more earnestly. . . . His sweat
became like great drops of blood.—Luke 22:44 NKJV*

Our bodies are complex things. God created them so that
when we get too hot, we perspire, and the moisture on our
skin exposed to the surrounding air begins to cool us down.
Sweating isn't always fun, but it's necessary.

Jesus sweated as he prayed in Gethsemane. Foreseeing the
horror he was about to face, he dropped to his knees and
wrestled with the knowledge of what lay ahead. In agony
he prayed, "Father, if it is Your will, take this cup from Me"
(Luke 22:42 NKJV).

When we fall on our knees in agony before the Lord,
laying out our questions and frustrations before him, he may
not give us the answers we want. More often than not, we
come away from our prayer time with more questions than
answers, questions that are meant to woo us back to God.
And so back we come again to enter his presence and wrestle
with our agony until we sweat. Until we finally say, "Not my
will, but yours be done."

It's like the first time you asked your parents, "What should
I do?" and they looked back at you and said, "What do *you*
think you should do?" And with that, the sweating began.

*Lord Jesus, even when the answers don't come quickly,
I want to continue to wrestle in prayer
until I know what you want me to do.*

Weekend Reflections

*L*ord, thank you for always hearing my prayers, even when I wonder if you are listening. Help me to remember your promises and remain faithful and obedient in those moments of doubt and uncertainty.

God has made provision for the salvation and deliverance of every man, woman, and child, but it is only granted to those who receive it. His heart breaks for every hurting child of the world, but he waits for one of us to minister love in his name. He longs to "heal our land," but he waits for the people called by his name to humble themselves and pray. He yearns to linger and talk with you if you would but seek to know him.

Your unbelief will interrupt potential blessings of God. Will you choose to believe today in the power of prayer?

Ripples of Reflection

- When you wait and listen in prayer, what thoughts do you wrestle with? What does this reveal about your heart? (see Matthew 6:6).

- James 5:17 tells us that Elijah "prayed earnestly." When was the last time *you* prayed earnestly? What were you praying about?

- God has chosen the prayer of faith to release his power. What might happen if you don't pray?

The Sin of Idolatry

You shall not make for yourself an idol.—Exodus 20:4

The word *idolatry* makes most of us think of the children of Israel paying homage to the golden calf. But we're wrong if we think this practice ended in ancient times or that it doesn't exist in today's "civilized" society.

In its simplest form, idolatry is appealing to something or someone else besides God. It says, "You can do for me what I cannot do for myself." Many people today idolize wealth or prestige. They let these things take precedence over everything else in their lives.

Another common form of idolatry occurs when people idolize another person, believing the lie that they cannot live without that person's love and approval. They may believe they simply love or admire the person, but if their lives completely revolve around the other person, if they consider themselves as having value only because they "belong" to that person, then they've slipped from love or friendship into idolatry.

God did not declare idolatry a sin just so he could hand down another restriction. He gave us this commandment because he knows the end of such a path. He knows there is no one and no thing in the universe that can fill the neediness of our souls except him.

Lord, I choose you, and I will have no other gods before you.
You are my shepherd; I shall not want.

Finding Your Way Back

*Repent therefore . . . so that times of refreshing may come from
the presence of the Lord.—Acts 3:19 NKJV*

Ever get lost in a busy place, maybe when you were about
the age of nine or ten? You were looking at something with
Mom or Dad close by, and the next thing you knew, neither
parent was anywhere to be found. Your heart probably
stopped, but you didn't want anyone to know how scared
you were. You took off walking, anxiously looking but not
finding them. You doubtlessly wanted to yell, "Dad? Mom?"
But you were too embarrassed, so you quietly darted about,
lungs heaving, eyes brimming with tears.

Then, among all the noise, came that familiar voice.
"Johnny! Suzy! Over here!" Relief flooded over you; you
probably wanted to cling to your parents forever!

The children of God lose their way just as earthly children
get lost from their parents. It's usually difficult to say exactly
when or how it happens. They are standing next to God,
something else catches their attention, and the next thing
they know, they're lost in an unfamiliar place of unbelief.

If this happens to you, humble yourself and call out to
God. Then wait quietly. In the peace of his presence, you will
hear, "My son. My daughter. Over here."

*Lord, sometimes out of selfish ambition
I have let my eyes be turned from you.
Then I cry out to you, and you save me. Thank you, Jesus!*

More Than Emotion

Anyone who does not take his cross and follow me is not worthy of me. —Matthew 10:38

In the intimacy of the Last Supper, Peter vowed that he was so devoted to our Lord that he stood ready to die for him. But around the harsh fire of scrutiny, he had a different emotional response. Sometimes our emotions may fool us into thinking we've committed ourselves wholly to God. For instance, we may show such sorrow for the sins we've committed that surely no one could ever doubt our sincerity. But manufactured remorse does not conform us into the image of Jesus. Emotional responses to sin are only the reactions of the human psyche. True conversion—genuine repentance, abject humility, and total commitment—comes only through Holy Spirit conviction along with an assent of the will.

This is not to say that emotional responses are wrong or improper. But we must be aware that we can have an emotional response without true repentance as well as true repentance without an intense emotional response. Repentance is more than being sorrowful—it is choosing God's way above our own. It is laying down our lives in exchange for his.

Jesus, I now set my mind to do your will, to choose your way, and to allow your life to live through me. Holy Spirit, come!

Crossing Over

*Whoever hears my word and believes him who sent me . . . has
crossed over from death to life.—John 5:24*

esus walked up to the tomb of his friend Lazarus and
stared death in the face. "Take away the stone!" he told the
mourners (John 11:39).

Now, if Jesus had the power to raise Lazarus from the
dead, he certainly had the power to roll away the stone that
covered the tomb. But it was important that the mourners
open the grave themselves. Mary, the sister of Lazarus,
explained their hesitation. "But, Lord," she said, "he has been
there four days!" (verse 39). Jesus knew exactly what was in
that tomb.

Inside of us there may be a tomb like Lazarus's—a place
where we have buried sin—and it is not a pretty sight. Jesus
calls us out of that tomb, but he will not remove the stone for
us. We must do that ourselves. And even though we desperately
want the new life he offers us, sometimes we hesitate. "It's bad
in there, Lord! By now it really stinks!" He knows. He has
said, "Though your sins are like scarlet, they shall be as white
as snow" (Isaiah 1:18).

The same one who said, "Lazarus, come out!" (John 11:43)
is calling to us now. Don't hesitate! Roll the stone away, and
let the Living Word shine into the darkness.

*Come, Living Word. I roll away the stone that has covered my
own personal graveyard. Speak your life into my heart.*

Who Turned the Light On?

*Many . . . believed in him because of the woman's testimony,
"He told me everything I ever did."*—John 4:39

*I*f you have ever been in the dark—real darkness—you know that when someone finally turns on the light, you're grateful, even if that light exposes things you'd rather not see! In the same way, when Jesus speaks to our darkness, even though his light exposes what we thought was hidden in our closets, our response should be one of gratitude, for now we can see the path to freedom.

The Samaritan woman at the well was shocked when Jesus, a Jew, asked her for a drink of water. But that shock was nothing compared to the rest of the conversation. Jesus told her, "You have had five husbands, and the man you now have is not your husband" (John 4:18).

You might expect the woman to fire back a defensive answer lathered with shame or anger. Instead, when Jesus revealed her sordid past, this Samaritan woman responded with gratitude. She ran to her friends saying, "Come see this man!" (see verse 29). Her actions illustrated the psalmist's words, "Thy words giveth light" (119:130 KJV). Jesus's words shone into the darkness of her life and exposed her sinful deeds.

Don't cower in the darkness. Open your heart and let God's light-giving, night-shattering words in.

*Lord Jesus, I willingly open my heart to the light
of your life-giving Word. I refuse to allow darkness
to live in me. I want to live in the light.*

Weekend Reflections

When we turn our faces to God for answers regarding a dilemma we're facing, or when we seek his counsel for a decision, he first demands that we destroy every idol. He can't do this work for us. If we have forged them, we must destroy them. This is the essence of repentance.

Idols have no power in themselves. But each thing we idolize is a foothold of Satan—proof that we already have been deceived by him and that he has already set up camp in our hearts.

Ripples of Reflection

- Think of an area of your heart you don't want God to see—an area you don't talk with him about—and resolve how you will open that "tomb" to his light.

- Idolatry is appealing to something or someone else besides God. It says, "You can do for me what I cannot do for myself." Are their idols in your life?

- Repentance includes surrender. What sins do you need to surrender to God so he can make them "white as snow"? (Isaiah 1:18).

Alone in Death, Together in Life

The man who hates his life in this world will keep it for eternal life.—John 12:25

Do you remember your very first day of school? Remember how your little heart thumped in your chest when you climbed on that big yellow bus all by yourself? Each step seemed like a mountain; maybe you wished Mom or Dad were there to hold your hand, but you knew this was something you had to do by yourself.

When school was out, you jumped off the bus and found those loving arms waiting for you. Our trip to Calvary is a lot like that first bus ride to school. When it comes to dying to self, no one else can do it for us. God will encourage us, but he will not do for us what we alone can do. Only we can crucify the flesh.

Is there a sin that easily besets you? It's up to you to lay it aside. Christ has already done all he can do. He laid down his own life as an example for you. Though many stood and watched him struggle down the Via Dolorosa, he still faced Golgotha alone. No one else could go to the cross in his place.

So we climb on the bus, struggle to climb those steps, and follow him in his death. Then, when we arrive at the end of our own Via Dolorosa, we find him waiting for us with open arms.

Father, you have paved only one road to life,
and it leads through the cross. I choose death
to my old life so that by faith I can obtain real life.

The Word of Life

That which . . . our hands have touched—this we proclaim
concerning the Word of life.—1 John 1:1

How often we may wish we could see and touch Jesus, as John did, to literally walk and talk with Jesus, to sit at his feet and listen. We cannot do that in this life, but he has left us something of himself: his Word. The Gospel of John begins with these familiar words: "In the beginning was the Word, and the Word was with God, and the Word was God" (John 1:1).

Upon each page of the Bible, his character is delicately revealed. Verse after verse declares his love for mankind. Again and again we read how he longs to fellowship with his creation, with his children—with us. The more we study, the more he discloses himself to us. And because of what Christ has done, there is no veil between our hearts and his glory. We freely look into the Most Holy and gaze upon his beauty and goodness.

As we study and set God's Word in our hearts, he fills our beings with himself, from glory to glory. As we come to know his Word, we come to know him. And as we know him, we know our reason for being. As we know our reason for being, we know life. Real life. The Bible tells us, "The words I have spoken to you are spirit and they are life" (John 6:63).

Oh Word of Life, thank you for revealing yourself to us.
Thank you for giving us something we can see,
hold, and embrace in our hearts.

Living Energy

To this end I labor, struggling with all his energy, which so powerfully works in me.—Colossians 1:29

Spiritual growth is a struggle as we continually face the old Adam in one way or another. But it's one struggle we should consider as a sign that we are growing into Jesus's likeness (see Ephesians 4:15 KJV). If there is no struggle, we may very well be coddling the old nature.

The courage to persevere in this struggle, thankfully, does not come from sheer willpower alone. God's resurrection energy gives us the strength and the courage to endure. It energizes our spirit beings as we "count ourselves dead" (see Romans 6:11). The apostle Paul explained it this way in his letter to the Romans:

> But if Christ is in you, your body is dead because of sin, yet your spirit is alive because of righteousness. And if the Spirit of him who raised Jesus from the dead is living in you, he who raised Christ from the dead will also give life to your mortal bodies through his Spirit, who lives in you. (8:10–11)

Paul wasn't describing the resurrection that is yet to come but our life now in the Spirit.

What struggle are you facing? Has God set something new before you that causes you to worry? Don't shrink from the challenge. Tap into the resurrection energy of Jesus Christ that "so powerfully works" in you.

Thank you, Jesus, for giving me that same power that raised you from the dead. I am now dead to sin yet alive by your Spirit living in me.

Jesus . . . Our Hope

But now is Christ risen from the dead, and become the firstfruits of them that slept.—1 Corinthians 15:20 KJV

When Jesus arose from the grave, so did hope for every man. On the cross, Jesus bore not only our sin but also every sorrow we might ever experience. He took all that pain into himself and triumphed over it. He descended to the lowest place, and today he stands on top of every mountain of despair that seems insurmountable to us.

And that, my friend, is hope.

You see, for Christians, hope rests in who we know, not in what our senses tell us. We may feel hopeless, but that feeling doesn't change the truth that Jesus lives. God's truth triumphs over everything else.

Are you overwhelmed with loss, with anguish, or with disappointment? Proclaim the truth that rises above the bare facts of your present circumstances—Jesus lives! See yourself with the disciples after the crucifixion, devastated and forlorn. Then run together with them from the empty tomb, carrying the news: he is risen!

Hope returns, joy springs up in you once again as you realize that death could not defeat him, nor could the weight of all the world's sorrow and grief—your sorrow and grief—destroy him. Jesus lives! He who has overcome the world lives in you.

*Lord, thank you for the hope we feel as we remember
what you have overcome—the hope that lets us
face the future with confidence.*

The Foolishness of the Cross

God in his weakness—Christ dying on the cross—is far stronger than any man.—1 Corinthians 1:25 TLB

The disciples deserted Jesus at the cross, probably because they feared risking their own necks by publicly identifying with him after his arrest, but also because of embarrassment. It was humiliating for them to have their champion, their leader, the one they had protected from the adoring crowds, hanging naked on a cross.

In the eyes of the world, Jesus's crucifixion was a symbol of weakness. The people knew the scripture that said, "He that is hanged is accursed of God" (Deuteronomy 21:23 KJV), and in their minds Jesus had become accursed. He was the laughingstock of the Jews. To be identified with him was to be identified with a silly man. A fool.

One of the most amazing things about the cross is that God took something that was declared foolish and made it the most powerful event in the history of the world. The one who was cursed and spat upon as he died became stronger than any man, stronger even than death!

There are still some who roll their eyes when they see a cross, considering it unsophisticated and unneeded. But the truth is, without the cross, we are doomed without our steadfast dependence on the blood of a humble Lamb.

Lord, I declare my whole dependence on
the power of the cross and your resurrection.
May the cross always be my glory and strength.

Weekend Reflections

God turned what seemed to be a humiliating ending into the greatest comeback the world has ever known. He can turn around your hopeless ending too. Don't be so sure your situation will end in defeat if God is involved in it! The truth is, only when we are at the end of ourselves are we positioned so that Christ can be glorified in us.

Ripples for Reflections

- In what areas of your life has God resurrected life out of death?

- How can you best celebrate the Resurrection today?

- Consider the energy it took to raise Christ's body from the dead. As you pray, visualize this resurrection energy at work.

Grace to Stand In

Let him that thinketh he standeth take heed lest he fall.
—1 Corinthians 10:12 KJV

*I*t's easy to cling to God's gift of loving forgiveness when we feel like wretched failures. In our misery, we recognize his strength and our weakness. When we're on our knees, humbly begging for forgiveness, we know we need God's gift of grace. But the truth is, we need his grace all the time. And we may need it most when we're standing at the finish line, claiming our accomplishments as our own work instead of God's working through us. It's then that we truly need his forgiveness and his love.

Standing there in the spotlight of honor, we may not be aware of our need for grace, but God knows better. He knows we can shine in glory only because of his providence; he knows we're able to stand only because of his grace. And we know it, too ... when the spotlight dims and the accolades turn to criticism and we finally come to our senses. Then we fall to our knees—fall into those patient, everlasting arms—and once again remember the source of our strength.

There, on our knees, realizing our need for his grace and completely dependent upon it, we are weak, but he is strong. And in his grace he will lift us up to stand again.

Heavenly Father, let me always be aware of your grace. Even in my overconfidence help me to remember your faithfulness.

Do I Have to Stand Up?

By [Christ] also we have access by faith into this grace wherein we stand.—Romans 5:2 KJV

When we're feeling inadequate and unworthy, it may feel more appropriate to kneel in God's grace than to stand with our heads upright. There may even be times, after we've stumbled off his path, that we wish we could show our contrition by crawling to him and lying on our faces until we earn his favor once again. Yes, sometimes that would be easier than going to the cross, beholding the suffering Christ, and standing there expectantly . . . accepting his forgiveness and grace.

But standing is the stance he has chosen for us. To come to him any other way says that his grace is not enough. Therefore, when we are buffeted and weary from fighting the world's temptations, when we feel like failures, we do not resort to collapsing on our faces in self-pity. Instead, we "put on the full armor of God, so that . . . [we] may be able to stand [our] ground, and after [we] have done everything, to stand" (Ephesians 6:13).

That is it. We just keep on standing. In his grace and in his armor, we stand, and his grace holds us up until our courage returns, and once again we not only can stand, but we can fight in God's power and might "when the evil day comes."

Father, thank you for lifting me up so I stand
before you despite my failures. Let me glory
in the power of your cross and your grace.

Empty-Handed

*In him and through faith in him we may approach God with
freedom and confidence.—Ephesians 3:12*

How do you approach God? Are you cowering, trembling
in fear of what he might say? Or are you hopeful that because
of your works of righteousness, this time God will be proud
of you? When you approach God in either of these ways,
you stand on the foundation of your own abilities—your
weaknesses or your strengths.

Even as firm believers in grace, too often we still find
ourselves trusting in our own achievements. Perhaps we
mistakenly think that our faithful devotion will give us
quicker access into his presence when, in truth, the only
thing that makes us worthy to stand before him is the
blood of Christ. While our spiritual exercises put us in the
place where the Holy Spirit can move and work in us more
freely, they're not the thing that gives us the right to stand
confidently before him.

God yearns for us to come to him. But we must come
empty-handed, boasting of nothing but the grace of our
Lord, resisting the temptation to gather up our golden
achievements and run to him thinking, *Now he will accept
me.* We please the Lord by our obedience and faithfulness,
but his acceptance of us is based on nothing less than the
holy blood of Jesus.

> *Father, I come, resisting the temptation to list
> the reasons why you should accept me. I trust
> that your grace is sufficient for me, just as I am.*

Unlimited Patience

I was shown mercy so that in me, the worst of sinners, Christ Jesus might display his unlimited patience.—1 Timothy 1:16

Once met a young man who told me, "I just can't live the Christian life. I don't have what it takes to be that good."

I assured him he was exactly right! Not one of us has, in ourselves, what it takes to "live the life"; that is why we need a savior. Face it. If we could do it by ourselves, there would be no need for Jesus. But we can't. That's why he came to earth—to empower us to do what we could not do on our own.

Even when we continue to wrestle with old habits, bad attitudes, and jaded hearts, God's love for us never wavers. Our weakness makes God's unlimited patience all the more evident. The apostle Paul, including himself among those who tried God's patience, said he was shown mercy as "an example for those who would believe in Him for eternal life" (1 Timothy 1:16 NASB). That idea was reinforced by Peter, another believer who had stumbled. He wrote, "Bear in mind that our Lord's patience means salvation, just as our dear brother Paul also wrote you with the wisdom that God gave him" (2 Peter 3:15).

Oh God, you never give up on us but have high hopes for our success. Your Spirit working in us causes us to talk, walk, and act like you.

Finding Grace

. . . so that we may receive mercy and find grace to help us in our time of need.—Hebrews 4:16

Grace is an attribute of God's character, a part of who he is. He does not create grace when we need it; instead, it is constantly available in him. Grace is something we simply find as we approach his presence. Mercy, on the other hand, is something we can ask for.

As children we learn how to obtain mercy by various ways, even by deception, so that we can sometimes bypass the discipline that is rightfully ours. A good parent may grant mercy when necessary, but his or her love and grace will remain constant, even in light of a child's disobedience.

Similarly, we do not ask God to love us; he just does. There is no need to ask for grace; it's just there. The only condition is that we approach God's throne and find it. And we also find another gift there: righteousness. It is this righteousness that gives us the ability to stand before the throne with confidence, boldly confident that God knows us and loves us.

Father, I'm ever grateful for your abundant gift of grace that awaits me at your throne. In all my seeking, let me long for what you long to give me.

Weekend Reflections

Grace is a daily need. It's not something we use only at the point of the born-again experience. And it's so much more than words from a religious creed. It is part of a theology that Oswald Chambers described as "immensely practical." Yes, it is by grace we have been saved, but it is also in grace that we stand (see Romans 5:2), and it is grace that helps us in our needy times (see Hebrews 4:16).

Ripples of Reflection

- Dietrich Bonhoeffer said grace is free, but it is not cheap. Knowing the price that has been paid, how should we walk, then, in God's grace?

- Grace is a gift, not a prize. What's the difference?

- How do *you* display the grace of God?

Are You Successful?

Be careful to obey all the law my servant Moses gave you; do not turn from it.—Joshua 1:7

*M*any people think success means acquiring great wealth and having friends who pat them on the back and say, "Man, you've got it made!" Others think they'll be a success only when they've climbed the corporate ladder and acquired an impressive title.

Solomon, one of the wisest men who ever lived, said such goals are nonsense. He described these worldly endeavors and achievements as nothing but "vanity" (Ecclesiastes 2:11 KJV), "meaningless, a chasing after the wind." Instead, he advised us to pursue a nobler goal: to "fear God and keep his commandments" (Ecclesiastes 12:13). Being obedient to what God calls us to do, he said, is the only true measure of success.

We should not look upon obedience with dread. For most of us, obeying God's mission for our lives does not mean a lonely life devoid of material prosperity. Success can't be measured by sacrifice any more than by abundance. The Bible tells us that "to obey is better than sacrifice" (1 Samuel 15:22). Obedience doesn't necessarily mean sacrifice; it does mean being faithful to what he has called us to do. Whose success are you striving for?

Lord, let me find joy in obedience, living the fullest when I am faithful to my calling and my purpose.

Do It Now!

As the Holy Spirit says: "Today, if you hear his voice . . ."—Hebrews 3:7

Are you responsive to God's voice in your heart? "Today, if you hear his voice," how quickly will you act upon what he says?

Many of us may not act quickly to do what God says because we find it difficult to clearly recognize his voice. We spend more time trying to decide whether it's really God who's speaking to us than we do in acting upon what he's saying!

I recall pastor Rick Shelton's describing how a fellow Christian would often ask him something like, "Were you in a spiritual battle yesterday at 2:00 p.m.? I felt like something was wrong." The pastor's response was, "When that 'feeling' comes to you, don't wonder what the problem is. Just do what God says to do!"

God does not give us knowledge about a situation just for our information but so that we can act on it by praying, giving, blessing, or doing whatever is necessary within our means. Just think of the battles that could be won, the disasters that could be prevented, the tragedies that could be avoided if only Christians would be quick to act upon the word from the Holy One!

Is God calling you to pray for someone, to intercede on a friend's behalf? Do it now!

*Lord, help me see the needs I fail to
fulfill because of my hesitation to do your will.
Give me the strength to do what you want me do—quickly.*

The Best Way

The devil led him up . . . [and] said to him, ". . . If you worship me, it will all be yours."—Luke 4:5-7

When Jesus calls us to his cross and works to develop his attributes within us, we find ourselves arguing, "Surely, Lord, there is a different way!"

Sometimes his way is not the road we would readily choose for ourselves, but we follow where he leads us because we know that to become as gold, we must go through the fire.

Jesus knows what it's like to strive toward the goal by following a harsh path that's not of our choosing. He came to earth to redeem the world, but the way to that goal was the way of the cross. It wasn't the way he might have chosen for himself. In Gethsemane he even asked the Father if there was some other way.

Actually, there was another way. Satan offered Jesus the kingdoms of the world without the agony of Golgotha. The goal was right, but Satan's way was wrong. Jesus knew that the only right way was the Via Dolorosa, the road to the cross.

Are you willing to be obedient, to follow the Shepherd of your soul, without looking for a different way? If we are to walk with him, we must choose his way . . . the best way.

Lord, the obedience you ask for may seem hard in the beginning, but I know it's the only way to my destiny. Your paths lead to peace and joy.

Fill Me Up, Lord

He put a new song in my mouth, a hymn of praise to our God.
Many will see and fear and put their trust in the LORD.
—Psalm 40:3

I have counseled many Christians who have become disheartened because of their own weaknesses, disillusioned the first time they fall and continually struggling to be faithful in the disciplines of the Christian life.

In this state of self-condemnation and helplessness, what a joy it is for them to discover that it is God himself who causes us to be faithful. The apostle Paul said he is the one who gives us this desire: "For it is God Who is all the while effectually at work in you [energizing and creating in you the power and desire], both to will and to work for His good pleasure and satisfaction and delight" (Philippians 2:13 AMP). And who is eligible for these workings of the Spirit? Those who are empty of their own will—those who give up the worries and failures and inadequacies that seem to overpower them and fill themselves instead with the grace and goodness and power of God.

It is only when we have emptied ourselves of everything else that we can be filled with God. The more you yield to this emptying and filling, the quicker the Spirit can work in you. In the position of surrender and helplessness, God fills with strength those who ask for it.

Father, fill me up with your power to work
for your pleasure. I lay down my will and fill myself
with your will, your kingdom, right here and now.

There's No Use to Hide

The LORD said, "Yes, he has hidden himself among the baggage."—1 Samuel 10:22

When Saul was chosen by God to be Israel's first king, he became a changed man by the anointing of the Holy Spirit. What high expectations everyone had for their first king! But when Samuel called a town meeting to present the new king to his people, nobody could find him. God had called Saul, and the Holy Spirit had changed him, but when it was time for him to assume the leadership role God had prepared him for, Saul hid in the luggage!

It's hard not to laugh at Saul's behavior, because most of us have felt like hiding sometimes when we think too much is expected of us. Saul's story teaches us that just because we're terrified of doing what God has told us to do doesn't mean we're not qualified as an anointed child of God to do it! Our Father is persistent when it comes to those he chooses. If he says we're capable of the task, then he will give us the abilities to do it.

There's no use to hide, my friend. God knows your hiding place. If he has called you, he has confidence in you. So come out of that cave, get off that ship, climb out from behind the baggage, and run to his side. There is nothing to fear.

Lord, forgive me for running away from the work you set before me. I choose to abide in your presence and to work there. Where else can I go?

Weekend Reflections

There is no such thing as partial obedience where God is concerned. It's all or nothing. Partial obedience is rebellion (see 1 Samuel 15). When Saul withheld some of the spoils of war, even though he did it in the name of God, the prophet Samuel said, "To obey is better than sacrifice" (verse 22).

Ripples of Reflection

- Dietrich Bonhoeffer said, "Only those who obey can believe, and only those who believe can obey." How is your faith in Christ the foundation of your obedience?

- Consider examples of so-called "partial obedience" and their grim results (Saul's actions in 1 Samuel 15 and the actions of Ananias and Sapphira in Acts 5). How do these accounts affect your attitude toward faith and obedience?

- Have you ever obeyed at the risk of having people consider you a radical? What happened as a result of your "radical" obedience?

The Kingdom Belongs to a Child

Unless you change and become like little children, you will never enter the kingdom of heaven.—Matthew 18:3

Only those willing to walk as God's children will find themselves as inheritors of his kingdom. This was impressed upon me one day before a church service. As joyful and upbeat preservice music played in the sanctuary, a young man with Down syndrome suddenly, without warning, took off across the front of the sanctuary, leaping and dancing. In his simple way, oblivious to anyone else, he unabashedly expressed his joy. Watching the happy gyrations of that young man, I was reminded of the power and grace that belong to those who come into God's presence as children.

Oh that we could come before him with that same kind of freedom and simple faith! No work, no sweat, no struggle. Just an open heart of faith that looks up to the Father with full expectancy and total dependence on him.

God's kingdom remains out of reach to us when we walk into his presence with arrogance, leaning on spiritual maturity and pretending we have our lives all together. It is reserved for those of us who come into his courts looking up into his greatness and remembering our smallness. To us he extends his hand and says, "Ah, my child. The kingdom belongs to you."

Father, I want to know what it is to grow up as your child, taking delight in discovering your kingdom purposes. Take me there again, Lord!

Childish or Childlike?

Jesus, perceiving the thought of their heart, took a child, and set him by him.—Luke 9:47 KJV

We all want to know that we have significance, but when that need becomes a childish quest to be exalted for the sake of power and self-centeredness, we'd better brace ourselves. Here comes the fall!

When the disciples argued again which of them was the greatest, Jesus did not overreact, even though after all the teaching and training these men had received from the Master Teacher, he surely hoped they would be getting the picture. Still, he didn't throw up his hands and exclaim, "Don't you guys get it?" He did not rebuke his disciples for their desire to be great; instead, he revealed to them the way to greatness: "Whoever welcomes this little child in my name welcomes me; and whoever welcomes me welcomes the one who sent me. For he who is least among you all—he is the greatest" (Luke 9:48).

There is a subtle difference in the two words *childish* and *childlike*. But there is a world of difference—a heavenly world of difference—in the two words' meanings. To be self-centered is to be childish. To be Christ-centered, we must become childlike. Small. Needy. The least of all. "Of such," said Jesus, "is the kingdom of heaven" (Matthew 19:14 KJV).

Lord Jesus, expose the childishness in me so that I can grow out of it and become a child in your kingdom.

Don't Mock the Seed

"The kingdom of heaven is like a mustard seed, . . . the smallest of all your seeds."—Matthew 13:31–32

We didn't grow mustard when I was a kid, but we did grow corn. It was amazing to me then—and still is—how that small kernel can be planted and grow into a huge stalk six to eight feet high with several ears of corn, each with hundreds of kernels. Jesus said this is the way his kingdom works. From a tiny seed to eternal glory.

Don't judge whether the kingdom of God is among you just by the numbers. Numbers alone do not verify God's presence. Out of the smallest church may come one soul who will preach to thousands. Don't fall for the lie that God cannot work through small towns or businesses. From one worker in an unknown company may come a new technology that will change the world.

Don't mock the tiny seed. You don't know what's inside. From the smallest word of encouragement, the simplest explanation of the gospel, God may grow a tree of life that will provide food for the anguished soul and shade for the famished heart. He's done it before. Nearly two thousand years ago he planted a small tree on a hill called Golgotha. And millions are still running there to find healing and life.

Lord, what are the small seeds around me that you are growing? What spiritual work have I been blind to?

Bearing One Fruit

The fruit of the Spirit is love, joy, peace, patience, kindness,
goodness, faithfulness, gentleness and self-control.
—Galatians 5:22–23

There are various kinds of fruit of the Spirit, yet they are all balanced parts of the same whole. For example, joy standing alone comes across as brassy and even pretentious. But joy with love is pleasant and uplifting to those it touches.

Or consider faithfulness. Without peace, it would be fatiguing. But faithfulness with peace is nourishing and comforting. We faithfully endure through various temptations while remaining at peace about the outcome, joyfully envisioning our reward to come. As James said, "My brethren, count it all joy when ye fall into divers temptations" (James 1:2 KJV).

This kind of fruit will instinctively come as our roots sink deeper into the Savior. Unprepared and unrehearsed, it springs from us because it comes from the one whose life flows from God through us to his children. We don't have to strain or work or coerce it from us. After all, it is not something we create in ourselves. This fruit is his love, his joy, his peace, patience, kindness, goodness, and faithfulness, branching out of us to shade others with the richness of his kingdom. If we are abiding in him, growing in him, we cannot be fruitless.

Jesus, teach me to abide in you
so that I bear much fruit to your glory,
a thriving expression of your everlasting life in a lifeless world.

Forcefully Advancing

The kingdom of heaven has been forcefully advancing, and
forceful men lay hold of it.—Matthew 11:12

When we declare Jesus as our Savior, we must also declare him as Lord. The Bible tells us, "God has made this Jesus, whom you crucified, both Lord and Christ" (Acts 2:36). For him to be Lord as well as Savior means that we submit our wills to Christ, our Lord, while handing over our sins to Christ, our Savior, to be cleansed by the power of his blood.

Now, having a submitted will does not mean we take an apathetic, passionless approach to the kingdom, feebly mumbling, "Well, whatever God wants to do . . ." If we do nothing but sit and wait for the future to arrive, it will—but we won't like it!

The kingdom of God is not a happenstance sort of thing. It is a living and thriving force, moving forward to the heartbeat of God as mighty men and women get on board and advance with it. If we are to be a part of it, we must tune in to the heart of God and move as the Spirit leads and guides us.

Our destiny will not just happen to us all at once. It unfolds as we continually yield our wills to the Holy Spirit in the here and now, today and every day, allowing God to prepare us for what is coming, while achieving today what must be achieved.

Lord, I want to be a part of your forcefully advancing kingdom.
I declare my will to be under your Lordship.

Weekend Reflections

A strange kingdom, this kingdom of God. It can't be seen with physical eyes because it's not of this world; it lives in the heart of man (see Luke 17:21; John 18:36). Even stranger, the only way one can enter this kingdom is to become like a child. It doesn't matter how many earthly crowns we accumulate. They're worthless in this kingdom—even detrimental. Oh, and get this: the king died to pay for his bride, but now he lives again. And the promised bride . . . well, she's a church of millions.

This kingdom of heaven is thriving today, growing all around the world. Its armies are conquering not by swords and spears but by the spoken word and the blood of the Lamb. You and I can choose to be a part of it, or we can sit idly by and watch it move on without us.

Ripples of Reflection

- Since Jesus has said we must become as children to enter this kingdom, what implications does this have for you? What childlike traits do you need to aspire to?

- Jesus said, "The kingdom of heaven has been forcefully advancing, and forceful men lay hold of it" (Matthew 11:12). How are you laying hold of God's kingdom?

- God's kingdom is founded on love, while many earthly kingdoms are built on intimidation, fear, or wealth. What are some other differences between the kingdom of God and the kingdoms of this world?

My Desire, His Purpose

May he give you the desire of your heart and make all your plans succeed.—Psalm 20:4

On a recent trip, the plane had just pushed back from the gate and was heading toward the runway when we heard an urgent banging and knocking noise below us. It was a member of the ground crew who inadvertently had been locked inside the cargo hold. When he realized the doors had closed and the plane was leaving, sheer panic must have struck his heart!

Many of us may think of God's will the same way that crewman thought of the airplane that day. We may believe God is about to take us where we do not want to go. Some of us are sure that if we prayed, "God, I will go anywhere you want me to go," we would soon find ourselves on the next plane to Outer Mongolia.

Is God's will for us always going to be what we least desire? Such an idea makes no sense. After all, if there is no joy in going where he sends us and doing what he asks of us, will we be as successful as he desires us to be? Even when we can't help but dread what lies ahead, we must remember that he is working in us, conforming us "to will and to act according to his good purpose" (Philippians 2:13). He will not lead us into something we have not been prepared for.

Lord, I am willing to walk according to your purpose for my life, knowing that you hold my best interests—and my future— in your hands.

Beyond the Open Door

Behold, I have set before thee an open door, and no man can shut it.—Revelation 3:8 KJV

The life of the believer has been compared to climbing a mountain, walking a road, sailing the ocean, or fighting the good fight. Always, the central element in such comparisons is movement or becoming, as God works in us to "do of his good pleasure" (Philippians 2:13 KJV), bringing us from glory to glory.

This moving forward isn't always comfortable for us. After all, it is the familiar things that bring us security. We often oppose change because it pushes us into the unknown and requires us to evaluate and adjust to new situations. Moving into new circumstances requires us to judge what is familiar to us and discern whether the change will be a positive one. Without question, the major hindrance to forward progress is letting go of the familiar to reach for the unfamiliar.

What change is God trying to work in you? What revelation are you resisting because of your death grip on the old and familiar? God has set before you an open door, a fresh anointing, a new realm you have never experienced. But to enter that new world you must abandon the past and trust him to lead you safely into a greater power than you have ever known before.

Lord, show me what I have been unwilling to relinquish. I want to forsake all and follow you wherever you may lead.

Making the Right Moves

Let your eyes look straight ahead, fix your gaze directly before you.—Proverbs 4:25

What if we could be assured that every decision we make would be the right one? It's a nice thought, isn't it? But it's not reality. Inevitably, some people may not understand our judgments; some may even be hurt by what we decide. But every choice we make should somehow assist us in pressing forward toward the goal, toward Jesus Christ. We must ask ourselves, "Will this choice in any way impede or delay my becoming like him? Does it move me forward, or does it encourage me to remain in my comfort zone?"

Solomon shared numerous mottoes and gleanings of wisdom that can assist us in making a good decision. When he advised us to "fix your gaze directly before you" (Proverbs 4:25), he was telling us not to concentrate too much on yesterday or even on what has happened today. Instead, we must look forward and upward. As he said in another proverb, "The path of life leads upward for the wise to keep him from going down to the grave" (Proverbs 15:24). Our decisions should keep us moving forward in life, said Solomon, because when we stop, we begin to die. The way of abundant life is the onward, upward way, the way of growing, of becoming.

Lord, I thank you for yesterday and for today,
but I look forward to what lies ahead,
knowing you will guide me to take the best path.

The Joy of Relinquishment

Consider what God has done: Who can straighten what he has made crooked?—Ecclesiastes 7:13

Most of us have to admit that too much of our prayer time is spent listing our desires and advising God on how he should do things. The prayers that are blessed are the ones that seek the heart of God, that lift our minds into another realm and earnestly seek the will of God "on earth as it is in heaven" (Matthew 6:10). Such prayers literally bring the heavenly down to the earthly.

Don't beg God to do things your way, and don't try to straighten what God has made crooked. When you do, you set yourself against God. The Living Bible translates Ecclesiastes 7:13 as, "See the way God does things and fall into line. Don't fight the facts of nature." The Saul who became the apostle Paul learned what it was like to fight the facts God handed him. Knocked down on the road to Damascus, he heard Jesus say, "Saul, Saul, why persecutest thou me? it is hard for thee to kick against the pricks" (Acts 26:14 KJV).

Many times we feel the same thorny pricks that Saul felt but fail to recognize them. Have *you* felt a few thorns lately? It could be that you're walking your own path instead of God's. Relinquish control and fall in line behind Jesus, watching and imitating his every move.

Lord, I will not fight against you.
I empty myself of my own will to embrace your will, oh God.

It's Not Natural

You may participate in the divine nature and escape the corruption in the world.—*2 Peter 1:4*

Raised in a devout Christian home, I learned the "dos and don'ts" early in life. My schoolmates knew I didn't participate in certain things, but sometimes they would ask me, "Why not?"

As a youngster the only thing I knew to say was, "It's against my religion."

As I grew up, I learned more about the "why not." I learned there was scriptural evidence for what I was taught, so when I was asked why, I pointed to a scripture that said, "Thou shalt not . . ." Yet in a greater sense, that still didn't answer the question. *Okay, so the Bible says it—but why?* I wondered.

From my present perspective, I see a greater truth: I don't do certain things because they are not part of the nature of Yahweh, and I am one of his children. For example, he says, "Thou shalt not lie" (see Exodus 20:16 KJV), because it is impossible for him to lie. By being trustworthy and honest, I come to understand a cornerstone of God's character: truth.

Why are we commanded not to do certain things? Because they aren't in God's nature. So if you're asked "Why not?" just say, "It's not my nature."

Oh my Father, I am grateful that you do not lie, steal, or break covenants. Please, Lord, let your divine nature work in me.

Weekend Reflections

*I*n discovering God's will, we must first lay aside our own will. George Müller wrote;

> I seek at the beginning to get my heart into such a state that it has no will of its own in regard to a given matter. Ninety percent of the trouble with people is just here. Ninety percent of the difficulties are overcome when our hearts are ready to do the Lord's will, whatever it may be. When one is truly in this state, it is usually but a little way to the knowledge of what His will is. (*Bible Illustrator*, Parsons Technology Inc.)

Ripples of Reflection

- By the example of Saul's encounter with Jesus on the road to Damascus, we can see that not all opposition is from Satan. What opposition in your life may be a message from God?

- If we would find God's will in major decisions, we must seek to obey his will in the little things as well. What little things have you been neglecting to do?

- If you are facing a major decision, ask yourself, "Will saying yes impede or accelerate my progress in becoming like Christ?" What consequences might result from asking this answer?

Where Time Stands Still

Come with me by yourselves to a quiet place and get some rest.—*Mark 6:31*

*R*est. Just saying the word can sometimes bring tranquility. Often we don't realize we need rest until our eyelids get heavy and our bodies grow so weary that it becomes obvious to others that we have pushed ourselves beyond the limits of our endurance. In the same sense, we do not always realize our need for spiritual rest until we are at the proverbial end of the rope, hanging on to a few loose threads. Finally, we cry out to the Lord for rescue.

God wants us to find rest before we get to that place of futility—before we get to the end of the rope. He wants us to find rest for our souls in him. As we fall into his presence, our emotions and intellect cease their laborious struggles, and time stands still. He who stands on the sea of eternity gathers us up in his arms and holds us safely above the relentless pace of life's battles.

As David said, "Find rest, O my soul, in God alone" (Psalm 62:5). True spiritual rest can be found no other place.

Lord, teach me to find rest in you before I even think I need it,
to respond as you say, "Come with me,"
and to find serenity in your arms.

Falsely Accused

Cast all your anxiety on him because he cares for you.
—1 Peter 5:7

*H*ave you ever been falsely accused by those you love? If so, you know that nothing hurts more than having loved ones believe vicious lies about you. How wonderful it is when the record is set straight and the truth comes forward.

Many people in our world believe lies about God, their Creator who loves them. They portray God as uncompassionate, uncaring, and nearing the end of his patience. Where did these ideas come from? Certainly not from God! No, it is the enemy who paints a picture of our Lord with a long, accusing finger, saying things like, "When are you going to get your act together? How many times must I forgive you?"

We must set the record straight for God. The Word clearly tells us that we have only one accuser, and it is not our Lord. Our Lord is full of compassion. He urgently calls us to himself, saying, "Come unto me, all ye that labour and are heavy laden, and I will give you rest" (Matthew 11:28 KJV).

Our Lord is loving, compassionate, and merciful. Those of us who know the truth must set the message straight, "proclaim it clearly" (Colossians 4:4), as the apostle Paul did.

Father, I cast my anxiety on you. As I name the things I have worried about, I am giving them to you, thanking you that you care so much for me.

All Is at Rest

You will keep in perfect peace him whose mind is steadfast,
because he trusts in you.—Isaiah 26:3

*B*ecause time often seems to press in on us from all sides and our work is never done, we may believe that God must be in a similar predicament. With such an attitude, our prayers can sound like this: "Lord, have you heard the world news lately? You need to hurry and do something!" We look at the church and see its weaknesses, its seeming frailty, and we want God to fix it—and fix it fast.

But God is not up in heaven fretting, dashing about trying to see that his will is performed on earth. He is completely at rest, perfectly confident in knowing his plans will come to pass.

We get a clear picture of how God feels about our anxiety in the account of Jesus and the disciples out on the Sea of Galilee. While the disciples were frantically bailing water in the middle of a blustery storm, Jesus slept in the back of the boat. He knew what was going on, but he was not the least bit worried or alarmed.

Our God is the essence of tranquility. He never gets tired or weary. When you are worried and fretting over something, picture God in heaven, calm and assured, in absolute control of his plan for you.

I worship you, Jesus,
because in you "all things hold together" (Colossians 1:17).
You are in control, never stressed out and full of anxiety.

A Short Trip Home

The one thing I ask of the LORD . . . is to live in the house of the Lord all the days of my life.—Psalm 27:4 NLT

Home is a place where we are most comfortable being ourselves. There is no need for facades there. While our earthly dwelling is only a temporary address, our true home is in the presence of God. And getting there is as simple as a prayer empowered by faith. Consider taking one of these journeys home in the coming week:

- In rush-hour traffic, turn off the radio and speak God's name over and over until you hear his voice in your heart, replying with your name.

- Instead of going out for lunch with the gang, bring your lunch to work, find a bench outside somewhere, and invite Christ to join you.

- Visit a chapel or church after work, and sit and read a couple of great hymns out loud until the truth of their lyrics becomes like water to the depths of your soul.

After doing this a few times, prayer will become an experience you look forward to with increasing anticipation. The wonderful thing about all this is that no matter where you are, you're never that far from home. In fact, you can be as close to home as you want to be.

Lord Jesus, home is wherever you are. Help me
to find my way to you daily, learning to behold
you face to face and coming to you as a child.

Life Needs an Intermission

On the seventh day he rested, and was refreshed.
—Exodus 31:17 KJV

One weekend when I was in the third grade, Dad set me on the tractor seat with him as he plowed the area we were turning into a vegetable garden. I felt proud that I had helped, and Monday morning I proudly announced to my teacher that I had learned to plow a field. She drew in a quick breath and said, "You mean you worked on the Sabbath?" I stood there, dumbfounded, not knowing what to say, then quietly returned to my seat.

Times have certainly changed. I doubt that any child in recent years has had a conversation with his or her teacher like I had with mine. Of course, what my teacher did not know was that Dad was an accountant and getting on the tractor was not work to him at all. It was actually quite the opposite. However, I never forgot that conversation with my teacher and through the years have attempted to look carefully at what I do on the Sabbath.

We need the Sabbath. Jesus himself said, "The Sabbath was made for man, not man for the Sabbath" (Mark 2:27). We are not exempt because we are busy executives, full-time moms, or sports-addicted teenagers. There needs to be a time to rest, a time to review, a time to reflect before moving on.

Yes, God, I get too busy with life and neglect to set aside time
for rest. You have given us an example to follow.
Thank you for the Sabbath.

Weekend Reflections

John Bunyan said in his immortal *Pilgrim's Progress*, "I saw in my dream that just as Christian came up to the cross, his burden loosed from his shoulders and fell from his back and began to tumble till it came to the mouth of the sepulcher, where it fell in and I saw it no more. Then was Christian glad and lightsome and said with a merry heart, 'He has given me rest by his sorrow, and life by his death.'"

When we rest, we relinquish our burdens, refresh our bodies, and nurture our spirits. How do you rest? You *do* rest, don't you?

Ripples of Reflection

- If Almighty God rested on the Sabbath, why don't you?

- Life needs an intermission. When was your last one?

- Read Hebrews 3:19–4:11. What work is the writer referring to in verse 10?

Wings and Chariots

He has rescued us from the dominion of darkness.
—Colossians 1:13

Although God himself is never rushed to perform his will on earth, there is one thing he does rush to. He rushes to the aid of his children. Often he does not intervene, however, until that lost child cries out for help. He is not willing that any should perish, but he waits for us to use our wills to turn to him (see 2 Peter 3:9).

Not only has God rescued us from the dominion of darkness, but he also delivers us from excessive temptation, providing a way of escape from every threat (see 1 Corinthians 10:13). In Romans 7, Paul described the constant battle between flesh and spirit and then exclaimed, "What a wretched man I am! Who will rescue me from this body of death? Thanks be to God—through Jesus Christ our Lord!" (verses 24–25).

Like Paul, do you find yourself struggling to conquer the temptations that plague your daily life? Have you veered off God's path and now find yourself backed into a corner surrounded by your attackers? Cry out to God, and don't be surprised if you hear the rustle of wings and the rumble of chariots.

God, you are never too late. What an awesome God you are that you ride the wings of the wind!

Take Your Time; God's in No Hurry

He will not grow tired or weary, and his understanding no one can fathom.—Isaiah 40:28

God is never impatient for us to finish our prayers. Since time is relative and God is not confined to it, we can take as much time as we want to formulate our inmost desires and thoughts into words. Even if we were the best orators in the world and could formulate our thoughts into concise, articulate phrases and express ourselves quickly and thoroughly, it would still seem slow to him. God can take in data faster than any man-made computer. His computations and speed are infinitely beyond any known scale. Comparing our communication speed to his is like comparing today's fastest computer processor chip to an ancient monk laboriously transcribing Scripture in calligraphy using a quill pen dipped in an inkwell!

On the other hand, our Father does desire for us to develop our prayer skills. Jesus taught his disciples how to pray, saying, "After this manner therefore pray ye: Our Father which art in heaven . . ." (Matthew 6:9 KJV). But when we try our best and still feel as though our prayers are weak and trite, that's when it's time to step back, forget about trying to be eloquent, and simply pour out our hearts to him. He has all day and all night to listen.

Your capacity to hear and to know all things is too marvelous to comprehend, Lord God. All glory to you!

Must We Love Prayer?

These people . . . honor Me with their lips, but their heart is far from Me.—Matthew 15:8 NKJV

In the parable of the Pharisee and the tax collector, one man prayed a prayer of honest humility while the other boasted so that those around him could hear of his good deeds. Jesus said God only heard the prayer of the one who was honest (see Luke 18:10–14).

God is not impressed with our goodness; he is only impressed with our dependence on him, which is measured by our faith in Jesus Christ and him crucified. We can be so committed to the ritual of prayer that we miss the relationship of communion; we can become so bogged down in the tradition that we miss the transfiguration. His presence may be revealed around us, but because we are so committed to the form, we don't recognize the one we are supposedly seeking.

I love to pray, not because I love prayer, but because I love the one I am praying to. And it is in that time of laying out my heart in his presence that he reveals himself to me. That is what I love about prayer—that I talk and he listens. And even greater than that, he often speaks when I listen.

Lord Jesus, may I never let the form take the place of friendship with you. Let my soul yearn for you, the Person, and not just the practice.

Learning with Christ

Lord, teach us to pray.—Luke 11:1

How it must have thrilled Jesus to hear his disciples ask him for this lesson! Nothing thrills the heart of a teacher more than a student who is eager to learn. Then the heart is most teachable. Then the words sink deeper than the level of logic.

Lessons are so much harder to learn when we don't listen! Consider Martha, working in the kitchen while her sister, Mary, sat at the Savior's feet drinking in every word. The teacher was teaching, but only the eager student was privileged to hear.

Today the Teacher is teaching: "But the Helper, the Holy Spirit, whom the Father will send in My name, He will teach you all things, and bring to your remembrance all things that I said to you" (John 14:26 NKJV). Are we listening? Do you want to learn? Is the cry of your heart, "Teach me to pray"? Only those who have "ears to hear" (Luke 8:8) will hear what the Spirit is teaching.

Lord, teach me to pray. My heart is open.
I want to hear what the Holy Spirit is saying.

The Foolishness of Prayer

The man without the Spirit does not accept the things that come from the Spirit of God.—1 Corinthians 2:14

Either prayer is real or it is one of the craziest things a person can do. For us to spend time talking to someone we can't see is not normal, according to human reasoning. But it *is* the normal thing for the spiritual person. The part of us that cannot be seen with natural eyes understands and knows that prayer is real. Our spirits long for supernatural contact with the Holy Spirit that birthed them into existence.

In 1934 a man named Vernon Patterson, along with twenty-nine other businessmen, gathered on a pasture to spend the day in prayer for their city, Charlotte, North Carolina. One of the prayers Vernon prayed that day was that God would raise up someone from there to "preach the gospel to the ends of the earth." Later that year during an eleven-week revival with Mordecai Ham, a young man named Billy Graham walked to the altar and gave his life to the Lord. Prayer makes a difference!

The world says prayer is a crutch for the simpleminded and needy, but that is because the world cannot comprehend spiritual things (see Romans 8:7). How about you? Are you a man or woman who will stand in the gap today and pray?

Oh Lord Almighty, your Word is faithful,
and powerful things happen when your people pray in faith.

Weekend Reflections

Prayer without faith is ineffective, but the "prayer offered in faith" makes the sick whole again (James 5:15). We must believe that prayer does change things. As Richard Foster said, "It is easy for us to be defeated at the outset because we have been taught that everything in the universe is already set, and so things cannot be changed. We may gloomily feel this way, but the Bible does not teach that. The Bible pray-ers prayed as if their prayers could and would make an objective difference" (*Celebration of Discipline*).

Ripples of Reflection

- What really big dreams have you failed to present to God because of your unbelief?

- Identify any area of your life that you are not praying about, and explain why you are not praying about it. Can you work out a way to begin?

- The disciples asked Jesus to teach them to pray (see Luke 11:1). Ask Jesus to teach *you* to pray, and practice what he shows you.

What You See Is What You Get

Now faith is . . . the evidence of things not seen.
—Hebrews 11:1 KJV

What do you see ahead? Are you frightened by what looks like certain defeat? When you pray about some discouraging thing that's confronting you and there is no visible change in your situation, do you question God's purposes? It's okay to answer yes. We all wonder about God's purposes when we're in dire circumstances.

I believe there is much God would like to reveal to us but doesn't because of the danger the knowledge would bring to us. And sometimes our limited vision prevents us from seeing what he *is* willing to reveal. Often, just beyond our present difficulties lies the fulfilled promise we've been hoping for, yet our present predicament blindfolds us. That's when we must see our future with the eyes of faith. If we wait until we have hard evidence to believe, we are believing with "Thomas faith." Jesus said, "Blessed are those who have not seen and yet have believed" (John 20:29).

Only with the eyes of the Spirit can you begin to comprehend God's purpose in your circumstances. So take heart. Learn to look through different eyes . . . his eyes. Then you may see God's purposes just ahead, waiting behind that difficult challenge.

Lord, let me see things clearly the way you would have me see them, remembering that the fulfillment of your promises may be closer than I realize.

Speaking Life . . . to the Dead

He is . . . the God who gives life to the dead and calls things that are not as though they were.—Romans 4:17

When we think of God giving life to the dead, the first image that comes to mind may be Jesus standing at the grave of Lazarus, shouting, "Come forth!" But God also rejoices in giving life to those who are spiritually dead, emotionally drained, and totally hopeless. Countless people today are only a shadow of what God created them to be. They are dead because the life-giving light of God has not shined into their hearts. But God loves to speak his word into the darkness and bring forth life.

Thousands of years ago God spoke to Abraham, an old man whose body was as good as dead, and told him he would become the father of countless descendants (see Genesis 22:17). Later God spoke new life to common fishermen and told them, "Don't be afraid; from now on you will catch men" (see Matthew 4:19). He reassured the condemned thief dying on a cross beside him, "Today you will be with me in paradise" (Luke 23:43).

And today he still says to the hopeless, "You have a future!" He says to those overwhelmed with guilt, "Your sins are forgiven!" And he says to the unloved, "You are my cherished one." He still is calling "things that are not as though they were."

Lord Jesus, you alone speak light into darkness;
you alone bring life where death has been.
Right now I receive the truth of your words of life.

When God's Voice Is Unreasonable

Go, sleep with my maidservant; perhaps I can build a family through her.—Genesis 16:2

God made Abraham a promise: "'Look up at the heavens and count the stars—if indeed you can count them.' Then he said to him, 'So shall your offspring be'" (Genesis 15:5). "Abraham, I will make of you a great nation. Your offspring shall be as the sands of the sea" (see Genesis 12:2 and 22:17). For a while Abraham believed. But eventually the facts of life set in, and Abraham started to think, *I am an old man. Perhaps God wants me to do something to make things happen.*

You know the rest of the story—how Abraham heeded his wife's advice and fathered a son by her servant Hagar. Today when we see the strife between Israel and the Arab nations, we are seeing the result of Abraham's impatience, the enmity between Hagar's son Ishmael and Sarah's son, Isaac. Thousands of years later the world still pays a price because one man lost hope for a moment and yielded to the voice of reason instead of to the voice of God. Let's face it. God's ways often do not make sense to our earthly minds. It just didn't make any sense for God to wait until Abraham was in his nineties to make the kind of promise to him that he made. But we need to let God be God!

Father, I know your timing is perfect. Give me an undivided heart to wait for your promise without wavering.

The Blessing of Not Seeing

Blessed are those who have not seen and yet have believed.
—John 20:29

Sometimes it just isn't enough to know that God is with us. We've been taught that his very name, Emmanuel, means that he is. So why do we sometimes have trouble believing it? Why do we sometimes long for face-to-face communication with Jesus? Why, sometimes, do we feel so much like Thomas, the doubting apostle?

Certainly, Thomas's doubting was not a sin. But what did Jesus mean when he told Thomas that those who believe yet do not see him are blessed? Could it be that Jesus was saying that those who have faith to believe without seeing are blessed because there is no war within themselves? We Thomases always have to have a sign. We're always looking, always reaching for one more piece of evidence. When do our minds stop their endless searching and rest in the blessed assurance of believing what we have heard is the truth? Can we believe that the Holy Bible is true?

When we are convinced in our own minds and our hearts are settled, then we are, indeed, blessed. We are blessed with peace, knowing we need nothing more—no signs, no physical manifestations—except "Christ in [us], the hope of glory" (Colossians 1:27).

Lord, I want to be one who believes without a sign.
Create in me a heart that believes what you say
more than what I see with natural eyes.

Tell the Story Again

Tell . . . your son and your son's son the mighty things I have done in Egypt.—Exodus 10:2 NKJV

When my friend reads a bedtime story to his daughter each night, she always asks for a "Once upon a time" story. No matter what he is reading to her, he has to begin with "Once upon a time," or he hears loud protests. Somehow "Once upon a time" promises her a good story and a good ending.

In the book of Exodus, God said to Moses, "I am going to do these things so you can tell your children and grandchildren about it, so they will know of my power and that I am your God" (10:2, my paraphrase). God was giving parents for generations to come a "Once upon a time" story to end all stories!

Recounting what God has done in the past gives us hope for the future. Because he saved those people in the "Once upon a time" story so long ago, we believe he will bring us through the "wilderness" of our lives today.

Is your faith weak? Do you wonder if God will do what he promised? Tell the story again. Remember how God brought you through the midnight of your life? Remember when you had just about given up and God suddenly rescued you? Tell your children and their children so that you nurture their faith in God and rekindle your own.

Lord, I will not forget what you have done. I will tell the story again. When I look back, I see the work of your hand. Glory to your name!

Weekend Reflections

To live by faith is to live by what we cannot see. Hopeful believers are not discouraged by what they see, because their hopes are fixed on what is unseen. Though they can only see the physical realm with their natural eyes, they know there is another realm that is unseen.

Often we look at circumstances we have prayed about and are filled with despair because on the surface nothing seems to change. However, we must remember that in that distinctly separate spiritual realm, unseen to the natural eye, a host of unimaginable activity continues on our behalf whether or not we are aware of it.

Ripples of Reflection

- How does your certainty about what you *can't* see compare to your certainty about what you *can* see?

- What do you place the most trust in, what people say or what God says?

- Faith is being "certain of what we do not see" (Hebrews 11:1). How certain are you about what you believe?

Keep Rowing

He saw them toiling in rowing; for the wind was contrary unto them.—Mark 6:48 KJV

Obedience to God's will does not mean everything will go smoothly, that the wind will always be at our backs, and that the journey will be easy. Jesus told his disciples to cross to the other side of the lake, even though he knew the wind would be blowing against them. Despite the difficulties, they struggled on, because they knew they were doing his will.

Do not doubt that you are doing God's will when you meet with resistance in your mission. God has a higher purpose than what you see from your limited view. Let your motivation come from the joy of being in his service and from your complete abandonment to his will.

When the disciples cried out for help, Jesus hesitated to respond, and we don't know why. Perhaps he knew they were safe for the moment while he needed to pray concerning matters that were of utmost urgency. Don't despair if God does not respond when you would like him to. He sees you. He knows exactly where you are.

Is your life stormy? Keep rowing. Keep watching. Any moment now you may see him walking toward you through that lifestorm, and as you cry out, he'll stop and come onboard, and your storm will end.

Give me strength to keep on rowing and to do what I know is your will, Lord. Come onboard my ship, and ride with me until the storm passes.

Daily Winnings

Let us run with patient endurance . . . the race that is set before us.—Hebrews 12:1 AMP

If success is going to be achieved, often it will be achieved through many small victories—victories that in themselves may seem minuscule. Usually it is not the flashy feat but a systematic punch-after-punch routine that cinches the win.

Several times in the New Testament, we are exhorted to "stand firm" to the end. This means we must not waver in the daily fight. We must remain strong in our faith—believing that we are overcoming, not just that we will overcome; that we are winning, not just that we will win. God is able to do more than we can imagine, and today, right now, his power is working within us.

I believe the "patient endurance" the writer to the Hebrews spoke of calls for gratefulness when it comes to victories and perseverance when it comes to defeats. Think about it. To patiently endure speaks of resolve and tenacity as well as long-suffering and tolerance.

Stop and thank God for today's victories and achievements, no matter how small they seem to you. It is the culmination of a long line of those seemingly small conquests that will bring about the final triumphant win.

Father, help me not to overlook daily successes while pressing on toward the prize that is waiting.

Drop the Anchor and Batten Down the Hatches

We have this hope as an anchor for the soul, firm and secure.
—*Hebrews 6:19*

We're often urged to keep moving, to always press onward. But there are circumstances when the right thing to do is not to move on but to stand our ground, to not back down. In this posture of resistance, we need a foundation to anchor ourselves to. Just any old support will not do. We must fasten ourselves to a hope that is larger than life.

An anchor keeps a vessel in a desired area. An anchored boat may rock in the tempest and push toward the end of the anchor line, but the anchor brings it back to center. Our anchor is the hope we have in Jesus Christ. Our faith may waver a little from time to time, we may be pounded by the waves of uncertainty and fear, but our anchor of hope always pulls us back to a center of confidence and rest.

Sometimes we may feel like we are standing alone atop Mount Everest, holding on for dear life as the windy gusts make us shiver and shudder. Perhaps our faith feels weak during gales of difficulties. Our trust seems to be tottering on the edge. That's when we grasp for that anchor of hope and hold on with all our strength.

He is a hope bigger than all our fears and problems. He is our anchor.

Father, since I trusted you for the power to save me, I will trust you now for the power to keep me saved. Thank you, Jesus!

Press On

The LORD had said to Abram, "Leave your country, . . . and go to the land I will show you." —Genesis 12:1

One of the things runners learn early in their training is to not constantly look back to check on the competitors. Winners concentrate on the race that is before them, not the challenges that are trailing their every step.

When God rained down destruction on the cities of Sodom and Gomorrah, the angel told Lot and his wife, "Don't look back, and don't stop anywhere in the plain!" (Genesis 19:17). We all know the rest of the story, how Lot's wife looked back and was turned into a pillar of salt. What we don't know is exactly why God sent this command. Perhaps it was because he was looking for unreserved obedience.

Pressing on under the guidance of the Holy Spirit requires total trust. We trust that God knows the best path for us, that where he is leading us is the best place to be. Looking back with a longing for what was behind us steals from us the energy needed for the road ahead. It robs us of "the joy that is set before us" (see Hebrews 12:2).

Lift up your eyes to the joy ahead, the journey before you. What lies in the future can be much greater than anything we have ever experienced.

Father, I thank you for where you are taking me and the good work you are doing in my life today.

No Big Deal!

None of these things move me.—Acts 20:24 KJV

Not everything in our lives needs to be intense. Sometimes a nonchalant attitude is acceptable—even called for. To say "No big deal" in the face of adversity can be a healthy approach.

It is a pleasant thing to be around people who struggle bravely but refuse to cry over spilled milk. It's not so pleasant to be around people who, at the least indication of a ripple in their existence, throw up their hands and are ready to quit—and not the least bit hesitant to let the whole world know about their "tragedy."

This is not to say, however, that spiritual warfare is not a serious matter. There are aspects of the Christian life that cannot be approached frivolously. But the dramatic soul who wants to lament and wail for months or years after personal failure must recognize that the root of such a reaction is often pride. True humility accepts one's own weakness as well as the grace and power of our Lord. Yes, we continue to persevere, but we remember that we are loved and accepted by God in spite of our deficiencies. And so we learn to be gracious to ourselves as well.

Father, I choose to walk the walk of faith and not be overly shaken by circumstances but will seek to persist under pressure.

Weekend Reflections

The path of least resistance is not always the path of success. To move onward, one must break through what is comfortable and easy. The boundaries we accept as normal are often chains that hold us back from progress.

To lead others to a higher place, we must walk there first. The uncharted regions of spirituality where the power and grace of God will be revealed in greater measure will take some effort on our part to find.

God told Israel that the land of Canaan was promised to them. Prosperity awaited them there. The goodness of the land would belong to them and their children. God would go before them, be their strength, fight for them, and protect them. Still, they had a responsibility: they had to go in and possess it. Otherwise, they would remain in the Wilderness Inn.

Ripples of Reflection

- There are some things worth fighting for. What is holding you back from moving forward in what God has called you to do?

- Are you willing to do what you are asking those who follow you to do? How have you already walked there before them?

- When you feel resistance that keeps you from moving forward, how often do you recognize that it could be Satan's efforts to keep you from moving on?

Patiently Awaiting a New Perspective

Trust in the LORD with all your heart and lean not on your own understanding.—Proverbs 3:5

The old saying is so true: hindsight is 20/20. Often, when we look behind us, things that once perplexed us begin to make sense, and we can see a higher purpose in something that at the time was beyond our comprehension.

So often in our lives, we search for reasons why. We try to sort out and analyze our circumstances so they make sense. It's easy to trust God as long as we can understand why something is happening—as long as we can see the outcome.

But God longs for us to trust him all the time—even when things don't seem to make sense, even when we have no idea how things are going to come out or why they've taken a particular turn. He wants us to abandon this need to lean on our own understanding.

It's not always an easy thing to do, perhaps because there is no middle ground. Either we are trusting him with all of our heart, or we are holding back, reserving a portion of ourselves that still needs carnal reasoning or understanding. We may not always be able to see or understand God's purpose for us in perplexing circumstances. But we must choose to trust him anyway, knowing his plans for us will give us "hope and a future" (Jeremiah 29:11).

Father, you have unlimited sight and vision. I commit my plans to you and pray that you will lead me in the right way.

In God We Trust

He will have no fear of bad news; his heart is steadfast, trusting in the LORD. —Psalm 112:7

We put our trust in God. That is how our hearts can be at rest in a tumultuous society. Our trust is not in a nation, a national economy, or a politician. It is in God. If our trust is in people, things, or circumstances, it will surely fail. But trust that is placed in God will not fail.

Relationships are based on trust. How much we trust someone—how much he or she trusts us—determines the depth of our relationship. When we come to know God, we learn that we can trust him; therefore, our relationship grows and is strengthened in the process. Trust can only develop through time and struggle. It does not come instantaneously but through repeated dependence on God's faithfulness.

Do you really trust God? Are you confident that he is working in your life, that the center of his will is the perfect place to be? If not, maybe you aren't really trusting in God but in your ability to recognize a bad situation and get out of it before it's too late.

Lord, I have said I trusted you when it wasn't really true. But I am learning. Thank you for your patience with me.

It's Time to Look Up

Let us fix our eyes on Jesus, the author and perfecter of our faith.—Hebrews 12:2

We gain maturity by learning from life experiences and applying what we have learned. Real learning often begins at a "life experience" we think of as failure. It is here, however, that we may learn the most, because it is here that our choice for growth or hopelessness becomes apparent. We can give up (and probably never grow up!), or we can search through and reflect on the experience to discover in it the seeds for success. This is a difficult thing to do, yet for continued progress it is a must.

At the point of failure, what causes the most frustration? Often it is the loss of our independence and the realization that now we must look outside ourselves for help. At the bottom of the heap, we find where our dependence lies. We discover where we have placed our trust. And only then do we realize our true foundation—whether it is the sand of self-sufficiency or the rock of revelation knowledge.

As long as we are relying entirely on our own expertise and strength, we have no need for God. But at the point of giving up, we can look up and hear our Father say, "This is what I've been waiting for!"

Lord, please forgive me for the times I have relied on my own abilities and strength when I should have depended on you.

No Other Foundation

Who can stand in the presence of the LORD, this holy God?
—1 Samuel 6:20

We must never forget how holy our God is. The Old Testament gives many accounts that reveal this to us, including the scene at Beth Shemesh, where seventy men died because they looked into the ark of the Lord. Here the mourning people cried, "Who can stand in the presence of the LORD, this holy God?"

The grace of our Lord Jesus Christ is the only hope we have of being holy and attaining true righteousness. We can't do enough good deeds to make us holy. It's just a matter of grace. The Bible says, "He saved us, not because of righteous things we had done, but because of his mercy. He saved us through the washing of rebirth and renewal by the Holy Spirit" (Titus 3:5).

If this righteousness could be attained through doing the right things, the apostle Paul could have done it. But he couldn't. After he listed all his accomplishments in Philippians 3, look what he said about them: "I regard them as rubbish, in order that I may gain Christ and be found in him, not having a righteousness of my own that comes from the law, but one that comes through faith in Christ" (verses 8–9 NRSV).

Jesus, you alone are my hope, my righteousness.
You have sanctified me and made me a joint heir
in your kingdom. Thank you!

The Opposing One

*"God opposes the proud but gives grace to the humble." Humble
yourselves, therefore.—1 Peter 5:5*

God opposes the proud. What a heavy thought! We
certainly need to have God working with us, not against us,
so we must yield our need to be in control. We must invite
him to become the Leader, Guide, and Shepherd while we
become the followers, the students, the lambs.

Humility comes from a sense of total dependence on God,
a complete trust in his faithfulness and care. In contrast, when
we feel anxious, we are taking control. We're being bossy.
Proud. We are saying, in effect, "God, hurry! It's going to
be too late! Please hurry!" We are wishing a situation would
change from its present state to what it could be—from
God's timing to our timing.

On the other hand, if we are humble, we recognize that
God is in control and that he is greater than we are. Then
ours is a faith that acknowledges a bigger picture, a higher
realm, than the one we may presently see.

So we boldly cast our anxiety and worry onto the greater
one. We declare our dependence on him and fling away our
independence. What a joy it is to do so, to place ourselves
"under God's mighty hand" and to fix our eyes on Jesus, as
he lifts us up—in his time, not ours.

*Lord Jesus, right now I throw my anxiety, my worry,
and my pointless concern onto you.
I humble myself under your mighty hand.*

Weekend Reflections

This favorite acronym speaks powerfully about what trust really is:

To
Rest
Upon
Sure
Things

When we say we trust Christ, we are resting upon the surety of who he is and what he has done. Any other foundation is sinking sand.

Ripples of Reflection

- Lies destroy trust. Think about the importance of truth in a relationship with God.

- What are the sure things of Christ that we can rest upon?

- How was mistrust involved in the initial sin of disobedience in the Garden of Eden?

If You're Happy . . .

Let the righteous be glad; let them rejoice before God; yes, let them rejoice exceedingly.—Psalm 68:3 NKJV

Must Christians always wear a smile? Are we always supposed to be happy? To answer those questions, we first have to understand what it means to "be happy." And we also need to understand the difference between *happiness* and *joy.* Jesus didn't say we would always be happy. Instead, he said, "I have told you this so that my joy may be in you and that your joy may be complete" (John 15:11).

Happiness speaks of a condition determined by present events. Joy, on the other hand, is a fruit of the Spirit that is not contingent on our circumstances. Was the apostle Paul happy in the dungeon? Probably not. But was he joyful? Yes! Because his joy was not really his own. He said, "I have learned, in whatsoever state I am, therewith to be content" (Philippians 4:11 KJV). Contentment and joy work hand in hand.

Christians aren't always happy. But, like Paul, we can be joyful in all circumstances, because "the God of hope fills us with all joy and peace as we trust in him, so that we may overflow with hope by the power of the Holy Spirit" (Romans 15:13, my paraphrase).

Lord Jesus, thank you for your joy. Even though I may not always be happy, I believe your joy is still alive in me.

Joy for the Journey

The fruit of the Spirit is . . . joy.—*Galatians 5:22*

The Christian experience is not one continual, ecstatic high but a series of victories and struggles. This is why joy is so essential for our progress. We need joy to sustain us on the journey, to help us see the victory on the other side of the struggle, and to have courage to accept the rain, along with the sunshine, that God allows.

Joy, as part of the fruit of the Spirit, may come when we least expect it. It may appear in the heat of a spiritual conflict when we suddenly find ourselves rejoicing because of what we see beyond the battle. Or it may come out of a painful experience with such power that it overshadows the pain. Jesus said, "A woman giving birth to a child has pain because her time has come; but when her baby is born she forgets the anguish because of her joy that a child is born into the world" (John 16:21). It is incredible to think that a woman could actually forget so much anguish, but such is the power of this kind of joy.

If you are enduring a trial, focus on the joy to come. Let the joy of the prize that awaits you cause you to walk in God's power and might with renewed vigor and the Spirit's immeasurable energy.

*Lord Jesus, thank you for being my source of joy
without measure. Though trials beset me,
I boldly press on with a joyful heart.*

The Joy of His Presence

In Your presence is fullness of joy; at Your right hand are pleasures forevermore.—Psalm 16:11 NKJV

Just as there's a difference between joy and happiness, there's also a difference between joy and enjoyment.

The word *enjoyment* symbolizes limited joy—joy while you have something. When that something is gone, so is your joy. On the other hand, true, sustained joy—spiritual joy—is the outward expression of what is abiding within you. The apostle Paul described it as part of the fruit of the Spirit (see Galatians 5:22). This fruit is harvested by those who have died to self and have been raised to life through Jesus Christ. As the apostle Peter wrote, "Even though you do not see him now, you believe in him and are filled with an inexpressible and glorious joy, for you are receiving the goal of your faith, the salvation of your souls" (1 Peter 1:8–9).

Christ Jesus is our joy—right now and for all eternity. There's no limit on how long this joy will last. It's eternal. Nothing can take it away from us, for the Scriptures tell us, "We will be with the Lord forever" (1 Thessalonians 4:17).

Father, the real joy I long for can only be found in your presence. I will "joy in God through our Lord Jesus Christ" (Romans 5:11 KJV).

Take Time to Dance

There is a time for everything, . . . a time to dance.
—Ecclesiastes 3:1, 4

As we steadily continue on God's pathway, we can be looking ahead so much that we do not enjoy the moment. Think of the Israelites as they reached the far shore of the Red Sea. They had just crossed through the waters on dry ground and then watched as God released the sea to swallow up the enemy. Surely this had been a miraculous experience that brought awe to everyone involved. But if people back then were anything like they are now (and I feel certain they were), there had to be those "do it by the book" killjoys who peered over the schedule at that point and argued, "But Moses, we really need to keep moving. According to my schedule, we need to reach Elim by evening!"

While these people fussed and fumed, Miriam stopped the march. She "took a tambourine in her hand" (Exodus 15:20) and said, "This calls for a party!" Then she and the other women led a celebration of dancing and singing before the assembled masses.

The Christian walk is long and challenging. There will be setbacks and difficulties. But there will be victories to celebrate too. Don't forget to bring along your dancing shoes!

Lord, thank you for today, for the little joys you give us along the way. I don't want to forget to say thanks, Lord, for every gift you bless me with.

Rejoice Evermore!

Through [Christ] we have gained access by faith into this grace in which we now stand.—Romans 5:2

*O*ur joy comes from knowing that every day we are accepted and loved by God, not on the merit of what we have done, but because he loves us and has extended his grace to mere mortals.

I was reminded of this one morning as I considered my accomplishments of the previous day. After a rigorous schedule that began at 5:30 a.m. and continued until late evening, I was able to get quite a few things marked off my to-do list: prayer, exercise, proper nutrition, and ministry deadlines. The next morning I was feeling more than a little pleased with myself, marveling at the joy I felt, when I was prompted by the Holy Spirit to recall the scripture, "We rejoice in the hope of the glory of God" (Romans 5:2). Soon I was even more joyful, but this time it was not because of what I had done but because I had been reminded of his grace.

No one is able to stand before God's presence except by his grace. What fun it will be, someday in heaven, to rejoice together as we see how God revealed his strength in us in spite of all our weaknesses! Just as today, so it will be on that great day: "We rejoice in the hope of the glory of God!"

Father, I rejoice today! Not because of my accomplishments or success, but for the grace that is so evident in my life.

Weekend Reflections

To attempt to endure life without joy is a draining experience. As Nehemiah recorded, it is the joy of the Lord that gives us strength (see 8:10). How can we press on without becoming exhausted, dull, and sour? By fixing our eyes on the joy that awaits us . . . the dreams of celebration and the thrill of victory that glimmer in the distance. Without joy we are destined for burnout.

Ripples of Reflection

- Think of one of your greatest goals, and dream up a creative way to celebrate when you reach it.

- God rejoices too. Search a concordance for the word *rejoice*, and find what God rejoices about. How do you have joy in the same things he does?

- God commanded his covenant people to have times of rejoicing (see Deuteronomy 16:13). When was the last time you set aside some time for joy?

Moving Forward

A little yeast works through the whole batch of dough.
—Galatians 5:9

The writer to the Hebrews advised us to "throw off everything that hinders and the sin that so easily entangles, and let us run with perseverance the race marked out for us" (12:1). When we get rid of all the little hindrances that hold us back from Christlike behavior, it will be easier to throw off the bigger sin that tangles us up.

One way to overcome "everything that hinders" is to begin our day with thankful hearts, to "enter his gates with thanksgiving" (Psalm 100:4). Then, throughout the day, we must be mindful of our attitudes. Small, positive decisions we make can have a domino effect just as much as negative thoughts and decisions can snowball into an avalanche of problems. We need to keep our thankful hearts beating all day long, thinking of everything we can be thankful for, no matter how trivial it may seem.

Then, from that first positive step, "let us run with perseverance." As we replace bitterness and fear with thankfulness, as we throw off those things that hinder, the sin or problem that "so easily entangles" us will fall away, and we will once again enjoy the victorious life God wants us to have.

Lord Jesus, I know your power will become greater in my life as
I cast off the entangling problems that hinder me
from what matters most.

Maintenance and Preservation

Do not neglect your gift, which was given you.
—1 Timothy 4:14

*W*ith a gift comes responsibility, whether it be spiritual or physical. The more valuable something is, the more maintenance, protection, and preservation it needs. We are wrong to think that because of God's grace we bear no responsibility for spiritual gifts, that God will simply take care of everything with no effort required on our part. He certainly is there to assist us, but he will not do what we are able to do—in this case, to devote ourselves to study, prayer, and worship.

"Do not neglect your gift," the apostle said. The opposite of neglect is maintain. Thus, the instructions might be understood as "Maintain the gift that is in you." Paul was reminding Timothy that he was to be a steward of what had been placed in him by God. Now it was his own responsibility to care for this spiritual heirloom.

Like Timothy, you have been entrusted with precious gifts. These gifts will not be used to their fullest unless you fulfill your responsibility to give them the proper maintenance and care. Listen to God; he will tell you what to do. After all, he's the manufacturer. He wrote the owner's manual.

Lord, you have given me valuable gifts to care for. Help me to be aware of my responsibilities. I am listening for your instructions.

In Training

Train yourself to be godly.—1 Timothy 4:7

Ask athletes training for major competitions if they enjoy all the discipline of practice and preparing, and most of them will answer with an unequivocal *No!* The daily regimen these athletes must go through gets dull and boring. But the anticipated joy of winning keeps them pressing forward.

The same is true in the spiritual realm. As the writer of Hebrews said, "No discipline seems pleasant at the time, but painful" (12:11). Somewhere along the way Christians have been misled into thinking that all spiritual exercise should be delightful, when in fact much of it is fairly ordinary. Not all prayer feels anointed. Not all worship seems heavenly. But does that mean it is not effective? No. Often the heavenly and anointed feelings come later when, as the writer continued, "it produces a harvest of righteousness and peace" (12:11).

We should make every effort to keep our spiritual disciplines spontaneous and spirited, but even when the results are not readily seen, we hold on to the promise of our glorious life to come. And we continue our training so that we might rule and reign with him someday in his heavenly kingdom.

Lord, I'm glad you hear me even when I don't feel anything.
I'm grateful that your Word is working in me
even if I don't see the evidence.

From the Natural to the Supernatural

God can do what men can't!—Luke 18:27 TLB

We should not ask God to do for us what he has given us the ability to do for ourselves. For example, we should not ask him to keep poverty away from us if we are not trying to make an honest living. We shouldn't expect God to miraculously keep our marriages intact if we do not treat our spouses with respect and follow the commands of Ephesians 5:22–33. God expects us to do what we know to do first, then he steps in and does what we cannot do.

The supernatural comes into operation only when the natural is functioning properly: obedience first, then the supernatural. It works the way Paul described his ministering to the Corinthian church: "I planted the seed, Apollos watered it, but God made it grow" (1 Corinthians 3:6). It was God who activated the miracle of growth. If we want God to activate the miraculous, we must activate the natural.

The prayer of faith is the trigger that releases God's power. We pray and God does the work. We do what we are able to do, then we turn the rest over to God. Even when we do not see him working, we have faith that he is.

Lord, I will not live as a victim the rest of my life but will do what I can do and wait for you to do the impossible.

The Right Place at the Right Time

The Lord said unto him, Arise, and go into the city, and it shall be told thee what thou must do.—Acts 9:6 KJV

To be able to hear God's voice, we may have to take a step of obedience first to get to the place where God can speak to us—or rather where we can truly listen to him. In the verse above, Saul heard God's voice from heaven telling him to arise and go into the city for further instructions. Maybe Saul wondered why God didn't just go ahead and tell him what he needed to know right then and there while he had Saul's attention.

I think Paul's repositioning—and ours—is part of our spiritual growth. God does not tell us everything we need to know right here and now. He knows there is a proper place and a proper time for revelation, for instruction.

And how do we find that perfect place and time? Through prayerfully seeking his will and striving to obey it. Our obedience, in itself, does not bring the blessing, but it brings us to the position where God can bless us and revolutionize us.

If sometimes your spiritual growth seems to have slowed down, don't stop praying. Remain in obedience. God may be waiting for you to reposition yourself to that right place at the right time so that he can bring about a radical change in your life.

Father, teach me to act quickly, to position myself where you can move and work in me to transform me into your likeness.

Weekend Reflections

Often it's the little things that are done consistently that make the greatest impact. As Samuel Smiles said, "Sow a thought, reap an action. Sow an action, reap a habit. Sow a habit, reap a character." What a principle! Thought leads to action, action leads to habit, and habit leads to character. There is nothing that replaces consistent discipline.

Ripples of Reflection

- A child without discipline will not mature properly. Think about the similarities between the balanced discipline of a child and the disciplines of the believer.

- A tried-and-true saying is, "Change the behavior, and the feelings will follow." You can't change your feelings by force. What habits are you willing to change?

- When and how will you begin?

The Supreme Purpose

I consider everything a loss compared to the surpassing greatness of knowing Christ Jesus.—Philippians 3:8

Maybe you have heard a comment that someone "is not serving the Lord anymore. It seems God called him to preach, but he's running from the call of God."

It may be true that *someone* called this person to preach, but most likely it wasn't God. The enemy uses all sorts of trickery to pull us out of a right relationship with our heavenly Father—even calling someone to the ministry. But anything that's detrimental to your supreme purpose, anything that keeps you from being a child in proper relationship with the Father, is not a purpose from God. "For he chose us in him before the creation of the world to be holy and blameless in his sight. In love he predestined us to be adopted as his sons through Jesus Christ" (Ephesians 1:4–5). It was God's pleasure and his will (his purpose) from the beginning that we could stand before him "holy and blameless." And he gave us a destiny—that we would be his sons and daughters through Jesus Christ. This is the supreme purpose of mankind.

There will be times in our lives when God asks us to do something that we find uncomfortable. But never will he demand something of us that will destroy our relationship with him.

Father, I confess that my supreme purpose is to know you, to realize that I am your child. This is my destiny, and I receive it now.

A New Name

They named him Solomon. The LORD . . . sent word . . . to name him Jedidiah.—2 *Samuel 12:24–25*

From Abram to Abraham, from Jacob to Israel, from Solomon to Jedidiah, from Saul to Paul, God has always changed names. Since God's plans are often different from the plans of men, God frequently sends a new name to fit his purpose.

David and Bathsheba named their boy Solomon, a name that has its root in the word *shalom*, meaning "blessed, happy, prosperous." This was a name that Solomon definitely lived and fulfilled; there was possibly never a man who prospered like Solomon. But above this, the Lord had his own name for the boy: Jedidiah, meaning "praised of Jah," because "the Lord loved him."

Just as God loved Solomon and sent his word to him, so also he loves you and is speaking words into your life, into your heart, into your being. Are you listening? Are you living out God's ordained purpose for your life?

God sends his word into us, and we become a new creation, a brand-new person. We start over. God wants you to be reborn into the person he planned you to be from the start. He has said, "You should not be surprised at my saying, 'You must be born again'" (John 3:7).

Lord Jesus, show me who you have created me to be.
Change me daily to become the person you planned
for me to be from before my birth.

Moving On

Elisha . . . burned the plowing equipment. . . . Then he set out to follow Elijah.—1 Kings 19:21

When Elisha received his call to assist Elijah in doing God's work, he went back home to kiss his parents, showing his love for them and his thankfulness for their nurturing, then he left. His actions remind us that our call to God's purpose for our lives is a call forward. There must be a thankfulness for the past and then a time of letting go. But this letting go does not mean abandonment. In fact, our moving forward into our own purpose is the greatest validation of our parents' competence.

Elisha's actions also illustrate another principle. By burning his plowing equipment, he taught us to see that the tools of our past may not be practical for the future. God will give us new tools for the mission he is appointing us to.

When we are born again, we are reborn as new creations. The old has passed away. It served us well, but God is not into remodeling; he creates us as entirely new beings. As we allow this rebirth to take place, our old natures will have less and less power, and we will become more and more like Jesus . . . until we see him face to face.

God, I want to move onward and upward toward the prize of knowing you. I will press on!

Where Is Your Legacy?

You . . . are a letter from Christ, . . . not on tablets of stone but on . . . human hearts.—2 Corinthians 3:3

*W*e celebrated my parents' birthdays by hosting a dinner for them with family and church members. During the reception, guests told how their lives had been touched by the gospel as shared by my parents. It was a gospel, these friends said, that was revealed by my parents' love, compassion, and generosity much more than through mere words.

As I listened to the heartwarming, sometimes tearful, remarks, I thought how great a treasure it is for any of us to know we have impacted another life! When it comes to lifetime achievements, the ones that will endure will not be the financial or material accomplishments but the living memorials—men, women, and children whose lives are better because of what we have done. Maybe we taught someone to read or showed a neighbor how to grow things. Maybe we held someone who was broken with grief; maybe we showed others how to laugh at themselves. One way or another, we showed people our love. That's what the apostle Paul was saying to the Corinthians: you are my living legacy.

Where is your legacy? Will it be written only on a tombstone—or on the hearts of men and women?

Lord Jesus, I want to leave a legacy that will not pass away.
I want to lay up treasures in heaven
where they will never become rusty.

Proper Acknowledgment

In all your ways acknowledge him, and he will make your paths straight.—Proverbs 3:6

A perfectionist always seeks to do things the right way. But the ideal is to do the right thing the right way. God has a wonderful plan for each one of us. He is at work in us right now to bring about a divine purpose and destiny in our lives. Our job is to discover that purpose and work with the Holy Spirit to see it accomplished (see Philippians 2:13).

I suspect that one of our problems in discovering God's purpose for our lives is that we seek him only in moments of great decision such as a job change, relocation, or marriage. This habit is contrary to the spiritual principle. The wise man said, "In all your ways acknowledge him." This means that in everyday circumstances we must realize the presence of God. We must recognize that he is with us.

If an honored guest joins us at a meeting, we usually acknowledge him or her publicly. We announce, "We are honored to have Mr. or Ms. A with us today." In the same way we are to acknowledge God in all our ways. We recognize and acknowledge that he is with us in every decision, no matter how small.

Jesus, I declare you Lord of this day and every day, Lord of my next decision and every decision I make.

Weekend Reflections

*W*hat is the whole purpose of mankind? Is it to acquire wealth? (Can you name the five wealthiest people in the world?) Is it to acquire fame? (Can you remember who won the Academy Award for Best Actor just three years ago?)

Money is not an end unto itself, and fame is fleeting. Our real purpose is to know God. Everything else flows from that one goal.

Ripples of Reflection

- What are you doing in your efforts to reach your supreme purpose of knowing God more intimately?

- How are you, as Charles Spurgeon said, carving "your name on hearts and not on marble"? What lives are you pouring yourself into?

- It is said that you can discover people's values by looking at their calendars and their checkbooks. What do yours say about how you are fulfilling your purpose?

Hope Building

Those who hope in the LORD will renew their strength. . . .
They will run and not grow weary.—Isaiah 40:31

There is a hope beyond understanding, a hope that has its source in the Spirit of God. This is the kind of hope that catches the attention of others. They watch in wonderment and say, "I can't figure it out. How can she persevere under such a load?"

Such hope is conceived by the Spirit working within us, but it cannot be birthed in a vacuum. In his letter to the Romans, Paul made clear the prerequisites for this kind of hope when he wrote, "We also rejoice in our sufferings, because we know that suffering produces perseverance; perseverance, character; and character, hope" (Romans 5:3–4).

It might seem strange to most people to hear that hope is produced by suffering, which most people would assume is counterproductive to hope. But the truth is that there is no reason to hope without some level of suffering. As Paul explained, "Hope that is seen is no hope at all. Who hopes for what he already has?" (Romans 8:24).

This is why we can rejoice in sufferings. We do not rejoice for suffering but for what is being formed through suffering. We are thankful because on the other side of the suffering we will be better men and women.

God, I thank you for hope. As long as I live in you, there is hope for tomorrow, for you are the source of hope.

Don't Move Your Hope

He has reconciled you . . . through death to present you holy in his sight.—Colossians 1:22

Is it possible to be saved and still see yourself as God's enemy? Absolutely! This is what happens when we place our hope in our performance rather than in the hope of the gospel. When this happens, we've forgotten that one of the miracles of salvation is the complete change in how God sees us. When we step through the veil of Christ's body, God then sees us holy and blameless. He sees us in love as his dear and beloved children. This change happens immediately through the supernatural work of salvation. But our self-portrait, the way we believe God sees us, may not change instantly, or it may become distorted at times due to our wavering faith.

Only Christ's death and resurrection have the power to change God's view of you. Where is your hope? Is it in Jesus, or is it in something else? Only a steady hope in the gospel has the power to tear down the false self-image you may have of yourself, an image of being an enemy of God. Only a testimony like that, so aptly expressed in the words of this old hymn, shows that you know you are an esteemed child of God: "My hope is built on nothing less than Jesus's blood and righteousness."

> *Father, I repent now of placing my hope anywhere but in the gospel of Jesus Christ. I boldly confess now that my only hope is you.*

Words of Life

Simon Peter answered him, "Lord, to whom shall we go? You have the words of eternal life."—John 6:68

The words that carry eternal life can only be found in one place—at the feet of Jesus. We urgently need those life-giving, power-packed words, and they only come when we spend time listening with our hearts to our heavenly Father's voice.

God's words revive us spiritually, just as words of rescue encourage us physically when all seems lost. Tell a dying soldier that a medevac helicopter is on the way, and he can hang on until help arrives. Give a sinking ship's fearful crew word that a rescue ship is on its way, and watch them strengthen their resolve to keep their vessel afloat just a little longer. Let a wanderer lost in the wilderness hear the sound of searchers calling her name, and watch her make it safely down the mountain, following the sound of their voices.

Just as God spoke the earth and all its riches into being, he also speaks life into our hearts just when we need it most. Are you dying in despair? Lost in a sea of doubt? Wandering through spiritual wilderness? Listen! God is speaking a word of hope that brings new life to your heart.

Oh Father! Help me to hear the words of hope and life you speak into my heart. I will seek at Jesus's feet the words that bring eternal life.

Don't Close the Book Just Yet!

He will renew your life and sustain you in your old age.
—Ruth 4:15

Naomi's history, laid out in the book of Ruth, is the story of an incredible comeback. When Naomi returned to her hometown of Bethlehem late in her years after losing her husband and two sons, she told her friends, "Don't call me Naomi. . . . Call me Mara, because the Almighty has made my life very bitter" (Ruth 1:20). As far as she could see, the best days of her life had long since passed.

But God had something else in mind for Naomi. Her daughter-in-law Ruth would marry a wealthy businessman named Boaz, who would redeem the family estate and provide much-needed income for Naomi. Ruth and Boaz would have a son named Obed, whom Naomi would consider her own grandson, teaching and caring for him devotedly in her later years. This grandson of Naomi would be the grandfather of the great king David, whose descendant would be the Messiah.

Have you closed the book on your life? Do you have the feeling it's just about over? Your best days may well be in front of you. You don't know the ending of your "story." Only God does. Place your hope in him and be faithful. As long as you're living, God is still writing.

Lord, I place my trust in you.
I am looking with great anticipation toward the future,
knowing you alone are in control of my life.

Life Is Not Permanent, but Our Hope in Christ Is

If in this life only we have hope in Christ, we are of all men most miserable.—1 Corinthians 15:19 KJV

I remember exactly where I was when I heard the horrifying news that the space shuttle *Challenger* had exploded, and later when I learned of the Oklahoma City bombing, the deadly attacks of 9/11, and the space shuttle *Columbia* disintegrating in the skies over Texas.

This must have been how the disciples felt when they first heard the news that Jesus had been condemned for blasphemy and would be crucified.

Horrified thoughts and questions must have swirled through their minds: No! It can't be! It wasn't supposed to end like this! What about the kingdom of Israel? I thought he was the Messiah. Is this the end?

For those awful moments, time surely stood still, and the earth held its breath. But God had a bigger plan—a plan that would cause the kingdom of darkness to shudder, a plan that would turn Jesus's disciples' tears to shouts of joy. Yes, it was a different ending than the disciples predicted, but it was a much better ending, a conclusion that far exceeded their wildest dreams: a risen, triumphant, and glorified Christ.

Oh God, I place my hope in you, my security and my faith in your power to do immeasurably more than I can ask or imagine (see Ephesians 3:20).

Weekend Reflections

*J*im Wallis wrote, "Hope is the very dynamic of history. Hope is the engine of change. Hope is the energy of transformation. Hope is the door from one reality to another" ("The Door of Hope," *Sojourners*, April 1988).

Hope lifts our eyes from the present grief to the promise of tomorrow and causes us to look upward instead of inward, to trust in God and his delivering power. It empowers us to look past the present darkness to a brighter place. It gives us strength in times of weakness to press on a little further, a little longer, a little higher.

Ripples of Reflection

- How would you picture a person who has little or no hope?

- Have there been times when hope carried you through a seemingly impossible situation to a better place? Think about how powerful hope can be.

- Some people scoff at the hope of eternity. Why is this hope so important?

This Too Shall Pass

Momentary, light affliction is producing for us an eternal weight of glory.—*2 Corinthians 4:17 NASB*

Life brings change—sometimes for the better, sometimes for what seems to be the worse. I have a friend who says her favorite phrase in Scripture is, "And it came to pass." She rejoices in the knowledge that nothing on earth is permanent, including whatever troubles beset us. The worst calamity is a passing thing; new possibilities lie on the horizon.

King David understood this principle. In the most famous of the psalms, he wrote, "Even though I walk through the valley of the shadow of death, I fear no evil" (23:4 NASB). We may walk through the valley of death, but we do not dwell there. Instead, we dwell in Jesus.

Knowing what is permanent—our promise of eternal life with God in heaven—gives us the grace to endure the "momentary affliction." Christ is permanent—"the same yesterday, and to day, and for ever" (Hebrews 13:8 KJV).

Although your present "affliction" may seem permanent, it, too, will come to pass. Someday you may look back and wonder how things fell into place the way they did. And beyond that, when his kingdom comes, even those painful memories will be erased.

Lord, thank you for the permanence of your love and your faithfulness, which mean that when affliction is just a memory . . . you will remain.

Morning Will Come

From the rising of the sun to its going down, the LORD's name is to be praised.—Psalm 113:3 NKJV

There will always be moments of darkness in our lives. Midnight always comes . . . with all its shadows, worries, and fears. We find ourselves tossing and turning on those long, lonely nights, our minds obsessively sorting through possible solutions to life's dilemmas. Or the telephone rings in the darkness, a harbinger of bad news.

But here is good news: the night will pass. It is a temporary state. And once morning has broken, the darkness is dispelled.

The shadows are overcome by the brilliance of the sun. There is no turning back. Night may come again, but for now it is morning. As the psalmist wrote, "Weeping may remain for a night, but rejoicing comes in the morning" (Psalm 30:5).

No night can last forever. The sun will shine again. The birds will sing, and creation will blush beneath the radiance of heavenly beams.

My friend, rejoice with me. We know another kind of morning. The Son has risen! He is no longer in the cold grave. The gloom of midnight has been vanquished by resurrection morning's light! As Isaiah urged us long ago, "Arise, shine, for your light has come" (Isaiah 60:1).

Jesus, thank you for the promise of a new day—
for your mercies that are new every morning.
No night can overcome your everlasting light.

A Harvest of Godly Feelings

Remain in me, and I will remain in you. . . . Neither can you bear fruit unless you remain in me.—John 15:4

*F*eelings are evidence of the condition of our hearts. When we have thankful hearts, even in the face of bad news, we react differently than if our hearts are darkened with pride.

When we can see our feelings as nothing more than the fruit of our hearts, we can begin to control those feelings instead of allowing them to control us. As someone so wisely said, "We don't do what we do because of the way we feel, but we feel the way we feel because we do what we do." By changing what we do, it is possible to change the way we feel. When we change what we allow into our spirits, our feelings change. But it is futile to try to change our feelings by working on the feeling itself—as futile as trying to make an orange out of an apple.

The Spirit's working in our lives will be shown by feelings of love, joy, and peace. Don't think you can simply say, "I have to start being less discouraged," and cause changes in your feelings. Instead, allow the Spirit to work in you by being grateful, and by carrying out Christ's love in giving and sharing. Then you will reap a bountiful harvest of good feelings.

Oh God, as my heart is refreshed by your love and refilled with your will, it will become confident of the possibilities you can work in me.

Don't Forget the Benefits

Bless the LORD, O my soul, and forget not all His benefits.
—Psalm 103:2 NKJV

*B*eing able to remember important matters is an essential element of our success in our careers and in our relationships. But in our Christian walk, one of the keys to success is actually learning to forget some things while remembering what is important. The apostle Paul taught us the importance of forgetting those things that are behind us and pressing on toward the goal (see Philippians 3:13), and the psalmist told us what to remember: "all His benefits" (Psalm 103:2 NKJV).

It is important to remember the benefits of serving Christ, because the time may come when we are faced with trying circumstances that will bring voices of doubt whispering in our hearts, "Where is God? Does he care?" It is at those times we must not forget "all His benefits."

And just what are some of those benefits? David offered us reminders: "He forgives all my sins and heals all my diseases. He ransoms me from death and surrounds me with love and tender mercies. He fills my life with good things. My youth is renewed like the eagle's!" (Psalm 103:3–5 NLT).

Do a little mental housecleaning today. Throw away the things you need to discard, but don't forget the benefits.

Lord, I will remember your goodness.
Thank you for the future I have in you,
but thank you also for the benefits of serving you today.

Why Are You Sad?

"Woman," he said, "why are you crying? Who is it you are looking for?"—John 20:15

Peter and John had come to the tomb at Mary Magdalene's request. Seeing that his body was not there and thinking it had been stolen, they hurriedly went back into hiding. Mary, however, lingered at the tomb, crying her heart out.

Then she heard the voice asking, "Woman, why are you crying?" Jesus stood before her. He arose from the dead and appeared first to Mary as she wept beside his empty tomb.

Even today Jesus appears to us in our anguish. I have a friend who talks freely about the day her husband died unexpectedly while he was having minor surgery. She tells how immediately after his death she experienced a peace and love so real, she couldn't believe how secure she felt. Looking back, she knows it was Jesus holding her in her anguish. It was his peace, the peace that transcends understanding, that comforted her in her darkest moment. The psalmist wrote, "The LORD is nigh unto them that are of a broken heart; and saveth such as be of a contrite spirit" (34:18 KJV). Though God sometimes seems further away when our hearts are broken, he is actually closer than ever. Look up. Listen. Seek him and you will sense his presence in you.

Lord, when we hurt the most, you are nearer than ever, because you identify with our grief and adversity.

Weekend Reflections

$\mathscr{S}$ummer has arrived. This is the season of vacations, sunshine, and recreation. It would be great if there were spiritual seasons, too, wouldn't it? Think how we could prepare if we knew when we were entering the temptation season or the blessing season. But there is usually no warning. Living with Jesus means adventure and a bright future filled with never-before-explored possibilities. If you find yourself in a season of temptation, sorrow, or suffering, look to the future God has in store for you and know that no season lasts forever—at least not here on earth.

Ripples of Reflection

- What benefits does God have in store for you beyond your present circumstances?

- Your faith in future possibilities may seem unreasonable to others. What is your hope based on? (What does the Bible say regarding your circumstances?)

- Take a moment to consider what season you might be in right now. Think about how the different seasons have come to pass in your life.

Enemies of Intimacy

The LORD says: "...Their worship of me is made up only of rules taught by men."—Isaiah 29:13

Religiosity will drive intimacy with God right out of your life. People who focus on the religion rather than the reality of worship never really become transparent before God; they simply get caught up in the recitation of familiar prayers and pleasing music. They never pour their hearts out to God in a real way.

Look at the contrast between the prayers of the Pharisee and the tax collector in Jesus's parable. "The Pharisee stood up and prayed about himself: 'God, I thank you that I am not like other men—robbers, evildoers, adulterers—or even like this tax collector'" (Luke 18:11).

Meanwhile, said Jesus, the tax collector "would not even look up to heaven, but beat his breast and said, 'God, have mercy on me, a sinner'" (verse 13). The Pharisee's prayer focused on his fulfillment of spiritual duties, while the tax collector focused on his humble neediness.

Every moment spent in communion with God may not be an ecstatic high, but you should not be content to remain at status quo with an empty spiritual devotion. Enter your worship time as if you were spending time alone with God . . . with no one else watching.

Father, what are the enemies of intimacy that I have allowed in my life? Reveal them to me by your Holy Spirit so I can be close to you.

A God Far Away?

She came up behind him in the crowd and touched his cloak.
—Mark 5:27

As a child sitting in the church pew I often sang a song that urged believers to reach out and touch Jesus as he passes by. It was an inspiring song, offering hope in one sense, but I wonder now if it might have imparted a subliminal message that implied, *You'd better catch Jesus while he's here because he may not be back for a while.*

The erroneous concept that God is far removed from us can sneak into our thinking before we're aware of it. There was a time when Jesus did literally walk on earth, and to let him walk by without reaching out to him was to miss a golden opportunity. But now we don't have to wait beside the road or climb a tree to see the Lord passing by. He has told us, "I will not leave you comfortless: I will come to you" (John 14:18 KJV).

And he does. His being with us is not a matter of condition but of relationship. He is not just the God of crises, but he's also the God of calmness. Not only does he walk the waves of the tempest, but he leads us beside the still waters. He is "'Immanuel'—which means, 'God with us'" (Matthew 1:23).

Lord, even if I walk through a time when I don't feel you near me, I know your promises are true.

The Deep, Deep Heart of Man

Deep calls to deep . . . ; all your waves and breakers have swept over me.—Psalm 42:7

Scientists tell us there are areas of the ocean so deep that even though the temperature is below freezing, ice will not form. The pressure above is too great. Yet living things exist in those depths that can exist nowhere else.

The same God who created these great depths of the sea also created human beings, and like the oceans, he gave us mysterious depths. The Bible says, "The purposes of a man's heart are deep waters" (Proverbs 20:5). This deepest part of our hearts is something we have only begun to understand, yet it is a familiar place to God, our Creator. For him there is no such thing as unexplored territory. This is his dwelling place in us.

Our friends and loved ones only scratch the surface of who we are, even after years of knowing us, but in an instant God reaches the very core of us. He is not looking for a surface relationship but one of depth and intimacy.

God has given us hearts deep enough to know him (see Jeremiah 24:7). We invite him into our depths by accepting his love for us, loving him in return, and by obeying his commands (see 1 John 2:3).

God, I have heard your call to the deep places. The deeper life awaits me, and I will follow you there.

Everyday Christianity

. . . when you sit at home . . . walk along the road, when you lie down and when you get up.—Deuteronomy 6:7

*B*eing a Christian is more than enduring a Sunday-morning ritual and catching a few midweek services. It is a way of life. Jesus is meant to be an everyday experience. So why are we reluctant to let this happen?

I am convinced that one of the problems is that we think God is so busy and preoccupied with other things that he does not have time to get involved in our personal lives. A related reason may be that we are afraid to let God see just how pitiful we are as we wallow in our weaknesses. Both reasons are inaccurate.

God is never too busy for personal involvement. He is all-knowing. He sees every knee that bows. He collects every tear that falls. And when it comes to trying to hide our weaknesses from God, remember that Scripture tells us Jesus himself is our advocate, able to sympathize with our feelings of weakness (see Hebrews 4:15). Real change begins in us when we acknowledge Jesus's strength in our weakness (see 2 Corinthians 12:10).

Let us acknowledge God's perpetual presence beside us—when we sit down at home, when we walk along the road, when we lie down, and when we get up. He is never too busy; nor is he offended by our weakness.

Father, I want to be one who acknowledges you in all things.
I want to know what it means to abide in you
and live in your presence.

Knowledge with Experience

The love of Christ . . . far surpasses mere knowledge [without experience].—Ephesians 3:19 AMP

How do we know something that "surpasses mere knowledge"? This statement implies something impossible—to comprehend something that is incomprehensible. Yet that is exactly what the apostle Paul prayed for the Ephesians—that they would "know this love that surpasses knowledge."

We know that faith comes by hearing the Word of God, and we know that Christ dwells in our hearts "through faith" (Ephesians 3:17). But we cannot really know God's love by faith, not in the sense the apostle Paul spoke of. We know God's love by experience and revelation. We can believe in God's love, but to know God's love is something much more. It takes an enlightening of our understanding, an empowering of our spiritual senses, to know what is beyond knowledge.

This kind of "knowing" is not weird or spooky, but it is supernatural. It is what happens when we really come into communion with our heavenly Father, when we hear his voice and listen to his heart. In this position we are experiencing God's love, not "just" believing in it.

We not only say, "I believe," but we say as well, "I know whom I have believed" (2 Timothy 1:12 KJV).

Oh Father, let me know this love that surpasses knowledge—that I may be filled to the measure of all the fullness of God (see Ephesians 3:17–19).

Weekend Reflections

It's difficult to fathom how and why Almighty God desires to befriend us. Friendship is usually based on trust and common interests, and knowing ourselves as we do, it may be difficult to see how God could find either in us. But he has proven his love for us by the Cross and seeks to have an intimate relationship with us.

Ripples of Reflection

- How does an intimate friendship develop? How do these steps apply to developing our intimacy with God?

- Does intimacy with God frighten you? If so, why?

- While God loves the whole world, he does have a closer relationship with some of his children, and he reveals himself in a greater way to those people. Who do you know who seems to have this kind of relationship? What do you see in that person that makes his or her close relationship with God obvious?

In the Steps of Jesus

Whoever claims to live in him must walk as Jesus did.
—1 John 2:6

*A*s a child, did you try to walk in your father's footsteps? Do you remember how you had to stretch your short legs to plant your foot squarely on your dad's footprint without taking extra steps? Or maybe you recall trying to keep up with your mother's quick pace, exhausting yourself in the attempt. As human children, it wasn't easy for us to follow in our parents' footsteps. We had to wait until our legs grew longer and our stamina increased before we could walk the way our parents walked.

As children of God, it seems even harder to walk the path that Jesus modeled for us. But Scripture says that's the goal we strive for. We can't do it by ourselves. It is the Spirit who gives us this ability. And it's the Spirit who sets our pace, not other Christians. We must be content to take small steps, patiently waiting as our spiritual growth lengthens our legs and increases our stamina and understanding. Only the Spirit can teach us to walk as Jesus walked. The Spirit patiently walks with us, guiding our steps, giving us strength to get up when we fall . . . until we find ourselves walking in the footsteps of Jesus.

Father, I yield to your Spirit as he teaches me
to walk as you walk. Thank you for your patience
with my small steps as I grow.

Look to Jesus

Fix your thoughts on Jesus, the apostle and high priest whom we confess.—Hebrews 3:1

Are you troubled when you see the failures of those who call themselves believers? Rather than focusing on others' shortcomings, "fix your thoughts on Jesus," who was faithful on every account, fulfilling the mission the Father created him to do. It is Jesus—not our human brothers and sisters—who serves as our role model. We must keep our gaze fixed solidly on him.

We see how he was faithful and obedient to his purpose while he walked here on earth, and we are encouraged, knowing that he will be faithful to complete what he has begun and that he will not give up on us until his purpose in us has come to maturity. By clinging to this promise and fixing our eyes on him, we can have peace when the world around us is in turmoil and when daily stresses unsettle us. We make a conscious decision to turn our thoughts from the problem to the problem solver. As Isaiah said, "Thou wilt keep him in perfect peace, whose mind is stayed on thee: because he trusteth in thee" (Isaiah 26:3 KJV).

We look to God, completely trusting him and deliberately choosing to trust in his wisdom and providence and to not lean on our own understanding.

Lord, help me to fix my thoughts on you,
to turn away from the things that are beyond my control,
and to trust completely in your omnipotence.

Your Life or His?

*As the Father has life in himself, so he has granted the Son to
have life in himself.—John 5:26*

*N*one of us have life in ourselves alone. Oh, we're alive,
and everything on the surface may appear to be fine, but we
have no life, no spark, in and of ourselves. The only life we
find in ourselves is a cheap imitation at best. In contrast,
the life Christ offers is abundant and full of passion; it is a
conduit carrying the limitless love of God to an empty world
of brokenness.

This is why, as Christians, we must stand at the cross, taking
fellowship with Jesus's suffering and emptying ourselves of
the counterfeit. There at the cross the voice of God is heard,
and the "dead" can experience real life. Jesus said, "A time
is coming and has now come when the dead will hear the
voice of the Son of God and those who hear will live" (John
5:25).

Are you trying to find life from within yourself? If so, you
will soon find that you're "running on empty." Jesus wants you
to have a richer, more rewarding, more gloriously abundant
life than you've ever dreamed of. He came to earth, suffered
a cruel death, and arose from the grave so you could "have
life, and have it to the full" (John 10:10). So which do you
want? Your narrow, empty, self-focused life . . . or God's rich,
abundant life?

*Jesus, your abundant life is working and flowing in me.
Fill me up and let your love overflow to any heart
that I may touch today.*

Daily Bread

I am the bread of life. He who comes to me will never go hungry.—John 6:35

There is never a moment when we do not need Jesus. If such a moment comes, we cease in that instant to be God-dependent and, instead, become self-reliant. We stop looking to Jesus for life, and instead, we seek it from within ourselves.

Jesus taught us to pray, "Give us this day our daily bread" (Matthew 6:11 KJV), and he declared, "I am the bread of life," while assuring us, "He who comes to me will never go hungry" (John 6:35). We come to him for life itself, and there is so much more to this coming to him than the form and ritual of worship. We must come to him crying, "I look to you and you alone, Jesus! My help comes from you!" If we do, he will never send us away hungry.

But if we are full of ourselves, we say to him, in effect, "I have no need," even though the emptiness of our hearts is oh so apparent to the one who created us. Sadly, when we come to him in that state, he does not force-feed us. Only when we come to him humbly, acknowledging our needy state, does he become our daily provision, our all-sustaining source of life.

Father, I cry to you, "Give me the bread I need for today. I am hungry and needy apart from you, the Bread of Life."

In the Garden

Whoever does not love does not know God, because God is love.—1 John 4:8

Why did God create mankind? He knew what the outcome would be. He knew that creating a being in his own image and granting it the power to choose would be risky at best. Yet nothing else could fulfill God's desire to love a creation that could choose to love him back.

God is all-sufficient. He has no needs in the true sense. But God is love (see 1 John 4:8), and love in and of itself is virtually meaningless until it is given away. Therefore, if God does have a need or desire, it is to love. And oh, how he loves us!

He loves us so much that he left heaven and came to earth to dwell among us sinners. He loves us so much that he stood in our place—hung in our place on the cross—and suffered the cruelest punishment for our sins. Our sins! Yet he himself was without sin. He did it all for love—his love for us.

To need love is human; to give love unselfishly is Christ. To love as he loved, not basing the love we show on what we receive in return, is to exhibit a small part of the substance of God that he has placed within us.

We are loved, and we are like him. So what are we going to do?

Jesus, am I abiding in you? Show me what that means. Teach me to abide so that I will bear much fruit to your glory.

Weekend Reflections

"*A*bide in Me," Jesus said (John 15:4 NKJV). The word *abide* is rich with meaning. In most cases in Scripture it means "to stay or to remain." This understanding points us to the reality that Christ is not someone we visit on Sundays but someone we live in, between Sundays.

Ripples of Reflection

- How can we abide, or remain, in Christ and still continue our regular work and play?

- Name someone you know who abides in the Father's love. What is the evidence of his or her abiding there?

- What happens when you abide in Christ whenever you are tempted?

Hands That Bless

*When he had led them out to the vicinity of Bethany, he lifted
up his hands and blessed them.—Luke 24:50*

What a thrill it must have been for the disciples to stand near Bethany as Jesus lifted up his hands and blessed them—and then was carried away. Imagine what it would be like to literally stand before God in the flesh and have his hands lifted over you as he declared a blessing.

While God no longer walks this earth as a man, he sent the "Comforter," the Holy Spirit, so that we could constantly walk with God and know he did not abandon us (see John 14:16, 26 KJV). And although we cannot literally stand beneath Jesus's uplifted hands of flesh and blood, we still feel his blessings each time we enter his presence. God no longer walks this earth in a man's body, but he has raised up another body here on earth to do his work. In a glorious mystery, his church has come together as a spiritual body, unseen with the natural eye (see Ephesians 5:30–32), as well as a body of believers representing Christ to the world.

As his body, we have the power to bless one another as Jesus did when he walked the earth. Whose life have you blessed today?

*Lord, I want to follow your example and bless those around me.
Help me remember the power of words to minister grace,
and give me hands to bless.*

Remember Your Prison

Remember those in prison as if you were their fellow prisoners.—Hebrews 13:3

Once we leave the prison of self and sin, it doesn't take long to forget the misery we suffered there. Living happily in the land of promise, where freedom is an everyday experience, prison can fade into nothing more than a forgotten memory.

To appreciate freedom, every now and then we must have a vivid reminder of prison. We must remember what that old, dark, musty place was like. We must see it. Smell it. Feel it. And then, remembering how good it feels to be free, we must declare this freedom to those who need to hear it, those who are still imprisoned. Only then will we see God "confirming the word with signs following" (Mark 16:20 KJV).

We must bring freedom to the prisoners. As long as we talk about freedom only to those who are free, the gospel doesn't have room to work. There is no need for God to display his might and freedom until the good news is declared to all who are held captive in the prison of self and sin. Jesus was not afraid to do this work. He reached out to the imprisoned, and so must we.

Father, may I never forget the chains that once held me.
Thank you for freedom.
Thank you for the glory of knowing that by you I am free.

Light Up!

That was the true Light, which lighteth every man that cometh into the world.— John 1:9 KJV

I had a friend who lit up the room at any gathering she attended. Though she is now with the Lord, I still cherish her wonderful way of bringing out the best in people. She knew how to make a person feel like he or she had something to contribute when it was really her own conversation skills that kept the communication flowing.

I believe she was so likeable because she was a builder of people, a female version of Barnabas, the "Son of Encouragement" (Acts 4:36). It seemed to come so naturally to her. Her encouragement was never forced or coercive. She had learned that the key to loving people was knowing first that she was loved by Christ. Then, knowing that fact, she could tap into the glorious and enduring love Jesus has for those around us.

People loved Jesus because his love was not self-seeking. He brought out the best in them. He saw their potential and called it forth. His love was always directed outward.

How do some people light up the room wherever they go? They know how to ignite the light in others.

Lord Jesus, you are the Light of the world.
Please ignite the light in me
so that I can shine on others and bring out the good in them.

Still Water Runs Deep

It is the same Holy Spirit who is the source of them all.
—1 Corinthians 12:4 NLT

How deep is your river of belief? The strength we show in the toughest of times shows the depth of our rivers. God said he would "give unto him that is athirst of the fountain of the water of life freely" (Revelation 21:6 KJV). Yet many believers exhibit a life that seems shallow and is easily exhausted. How can we share Christ's love with others if our own reservoirs are dry?

If the life you offer others is of yourself, it will not be enough. The people you touch will walk away having had only a sip of refreshment. Their thirst will still be unquenched, and you yourself will soon be depleted. Only God, the Fountain of life, can offer living water. To get the living water—and to give it to others—you have to go to the Source: Jesus, the fountain from which all living water flows.

When you see believers who show courage when you would expect them to be fearful, who glow with peace when their hearts should be in turmoil, you can know that their rivers run deep—and that the source of their strength is the Fountain of abundant life.

Father, thank you for the gift of abundant life, the nourishment of living water. At your right hand are pleasures forevermore.

Have You Mocked His Face?

We curse men, who have been made in God's likeness.
—James 3:9

I have been with people who claimed to know Christ and yet would mock those of different cultures, openly displaying their preconceived notions and ugly prejudice gained through legend and gossip. What fools we are to think we are somehow better than others because we have a different upbringing or skin pigmentation, or were born in a different state or country! What fools we are to think we have any significance at all—except in God's eyes!

How can we who were dead and spiritually impoverished before God found us mock and prejudge those who are different from us and yet so much like us? More importantly, they were created in the "likeness of God." So when we ridicule others, we are, in essence, laughing at God's image. Laughing at something he created and died for. "My brothers, this should not be," James said (3:10).

To God we are all priceless! We're so valuable, in fact, that God gave his only Son to die for our transgressions. Why? Because of his immeasurable love for us. Because when he looks at us he sees his image, and it is impossible for God to hate something that looks like himself.

Lord, forgive me for the times I have not seen others through your eyes of love, rejecting them because of their differences. I "will" to love.

Weekend Reflections

The love Christ has placed in our hearts is for sharing; the grace he has covered us with is to be extended to others. As Christians we are the hands and feet of Jesus on earth. It is our privilege and responsibility to represent him lovingly.

Ripples of Reflection

- Do you know people who "light up the room" when they enter? Most likely they are people who love other people. How do they demonstrate it?

- If there is to be long-lasting fruit from our ministry, then the ministry must be motivated by love. Why do you do what you do?

- Jesus said we can literally love him by loving others (see Matthew 25:38–40). What will you do for others that will demonstrate your love for Jesus?

Seize the Day!

This is the day the LORD has made; let us rejoice and be glad in it.—Psalm 118:24

here has never been a day just like today. Nor will there ever be again. The exact combination of today's people, ages, weather, and places cannot be duplicated. For you—and for all of us—today is unique.

There is a Latin phrase, *carpe diem*, that means "seize the day." How often we let days go by, wasting precious opportunities that will never come again. When we're always waiting for that "someday" to begin a new challenge or adventure, wasted days turn into weeks and years, and eventually we lose sight of dreams and goals.

What is the thing you have always dreamed of doing or being? Begin today! Each day can bring you one step closer to your goal as you use every moment to its fullest. As the apostle Paul told the Romans, "The hour has come for you to wake up from your slumber, because our salvation is nearer now than when we first believed. The night is nearly over; the day is almost here" (13:11–12).

Let us awake each morning with ambition and discipline to live each day to its fullest, using each moment to further the kingdom of God.

*Lord, help me see the opportunities of today—
the people I can touch and the things I can accomplish
for the sake of your kingdom.*

Is Your Life in a Holding Pattern?

Ye have compassed this mountain long enough: turn you
northward.—Deuteronomy 2:3 KJV

Have you ever felt like your spiritual walk is going in circles? Do you have dreams for the future that seem to stay beyond your reach, while again and again you do the same thing you've been doing? If so, you probably feel like pilots do when air-traffic control puts them in a holding pattern, causing them to fly in circles until the weather or traffic is resolved and they can land. Several planes may be directed to hold at specified altitudes, circling until they're given instructions to move down to another altitude and continue circling, until finally the pilot works his or her way down through the stack and is given final clearance to land.

The book of Hebrews describes how God put the Israelites in a "holding pattern" in the wilderness for forty years because of their disobedience. Today, when we find ourselves in a holding pattern, doing the same thing we've done before, falling short of our hopes and dreams for the future, perhaps we need to look back and consider where we may have disobeyed. I believe God puts us in these holding patterns, not to punish us, but to give us time to learn and mature before he allows us to break out of the pattern and finally move on.

Lord, empower me to always choose the path of obedience, no matter the cost. I want to move forward in your power.

The Flower of Life

He flourishes like a flower of the field; the wind blows over it and it is gone.—Psalm 103:15–16

God compares our life on earth to a flower, a thing of beauty to be enjoyed. But no matter what we do for the flower, we cannot hold on to its beauty.

We pamper our bodies, trying to hold on to youth. But no matter what we do, youth smugly escapes our tight grip. The book of James compares our life to a vapor: "For what is your life? It is even a vapour, that appeareth for a little time, and then vanisheth away" (James 4:14 KJV). A vapor is impossible to grasp; it slips right through our fingers.

That's why the Lord taught us not to worry about tomorrow or to say, "Next year I will go here, do this and that" (see James 4:13). We are not promised tomorrow. All we have is the here and now. So don't say, "On my friend's next birthday I'm going to really show her how much I appreciate her." Go tell her now! Celebrate a forty-seventh wedding anniversary instead of waiting for the fiftieth. Don't put off the big party until age forty. Celebrate thirty-nine!

Today is the flower of our lives. Bloom now! Let the beauty of his grace shout out to the world, "I'm loved! I'm free! I'm alive!" Tomorrow may be too late.

Lord, thank you for today. I will open my eyes and seek to know what you are doing in and around me on this day you have given me.

Is Your Head in the Clouds?

Whoever watches the wind will not plant; whoever looks at the clouds will not reap.—Ecclesiastes 11:4

*I*f you're waiting for perfect conditions before you do something, you will never do anything! Or maybe you're honest enough to admit the truth. You're not really waiting for the perfect time or the perfect circumstances. You're daydreaming. Wasting time.

The work of God can seem mundane and unproductive at times. We lose our commitment, and our enthusiasm fades, especially when people ask, "Why bother? People get saved, but then they don't walk the Christian walk. So what's the use?"

In those moments we must not fall into periods of reverie where we do nothing but watch the wind and study the clouds. Our job is to sow the seed; God is the one who causes it to grow (see 1 Corinthians 3:7). Sow your energy into your job. Sow yourself into your children. Sow wherever the path leads you. The law of the harvest says that some of those seeds are going to fall on good ground and bring a great harvest. God knows which ones. He's working in them. Don't be frustrated about the others. Keep your eye on the path, not on the clouds and the wind. Look to Jesus and start planting!

Lord, help me to rid my life of idle daydreaming and procrastination, and send me into your field to enthusiastically sow the seed for you.

Is It Time to Laugh or Cry . . . or Neither?

. . . a time to cry and a time to laugh. A time to grieve and a time to dance.—Ecclesiastes 3:4 NLT

Why, exactly, do our feelings change? Sometimes we try to have a feeling we enjoyed at another time—a feeling of intimacy or affection or enthusiasm, perhaps—and we can't quite recapture it. The truth is, the harder we try to get a particular feeling, the more it seems to escape us. It's like chasing the wind. And the wind is unpredictable. It "blows where it wishes, and you hear the sound of it, but cannot tell where it comes from and where it goes" (John 3:8 NKJV).

Have you ever felt down and didn't know why? King David must have wondered the same thing when he wrote, "Why am I discouraged? Why so sad? I will put my hope in God! I will praise him again—my Savior and my God!" (Psalm 43:5 NLT).

David knew the solution. He exerted his will to do the right thing. He told himself, "Even when you don't feel like it, do the right thing anyway!"

You might need to will yourself to love or to care or to attack a job eagerly. David's advice was: just do the right thing, and the time will come when you'll feel like dancing again. Don't spend your time chasing the wind. Chase after God's will for your life instead!

Lord, I will praise you with my whole heart. I will myself to love and cherish those you have placed in my life because you love me.

191

Weekend Reflections

Tomorrow is fleeting, and the past is out of reach. Today is a fresh gift from God. The psalmist triumphantly declared, "This is the day the LORD has made; let us rejoice and be glad in it" (Psalm 118:24). Each day brings new opportunities, and each day holds the promise of mended relationships, deeds of kindness, or thoughtful expressions of love. Don't let this day go by without seizing the opportunity to touch someone's life for good or deepen your relationship with your Creator.

Ripples of Reflection

- What have you always dreamed of being or doing? What can you do today to take a first step toward making that dream a reality?

- Is there something you have been refusing to do or give up or act on? What step of obedience can you take today?

- Do you have your head in the clouds? Are you daydreaming instead of sowing seeds of love, kindness, and the good news of Jesus? Where can you sow God's seed today?

The Way to Abundant Life

[He] has given us everything we need for life and godliness through our knowledge of him.—2 Peter 1:3

In the business world, relationships become all-important, and we work hard to maintain a network of friends and colleagues we can turn to in time of need. That's the real motivation for relationships in the workplace: need.

In contrast, God called us into relationship with himself for no other reason except that he loves us. He doesn't value us because of our own goodness but simply because of his loving-kindness. And he gives us everything we need to maintain this relationship with him as well as the ability to live a life full of true joy and abiding happiness.

We achieve this fulfilling life as a result of our personal knowledge of God. Only by knowing him can we be transported out of the dungeon of hopelessness, out of spiritual poverty, and into the abounding riches of his glory. There, in his riches—in relationship with him—we find the essentials for an exhilarating life as well as the power to be free to grow into his likeness.

Father, true godliness comes from a right relationship with you, which provides everything needed to live a godly and abundant life.

If You Remain in Me

If anyone does not remain in me, he is like a branch that is thrown away and withers.—John 15:6

To remain in Christ as a permanent state is a challenge, even for the most devoted believers. To be in the world yet not a part of it is a constant struggle. Yet to survive, our reliance on him must become perpetual, not conditional. We must learn to abide in him in times of strength as well as in times of need.

He is the vine; we are the branches. Just as branches get their sustenance from the vine, so we draw sustenance from Christ. The branch separated from the vine withers, becomes brittle, and is easily destroyed. Those who do not remain connected to Christ become "brittle" in their spirits. They are susceptible to the enemy's assault, and they burn easily. Those who remain in the vine, however, are full of the sweetness of its sap, the lifeblood that gives them strength to withstand hard times. They cannot be burned, for they are alive with the love of God and have become a channel of this love to others.

Who is the source of your life? When you are in despair, who do you draw your strength from? Get connected to the Vine. Realize Christ in you. He is the source of powerful, abundant life.

Lord, teach me to remain in you wherever I am, wherever I go, always keeping you as my real source of life.

Knowledge Is Power

I want to know Christ and the power of his resurrection.
—*Philippians 3:10*

Why can one church sing a song of worship and generate a great sense of the glory of God while another congregation sings the same song and there is only hollowness? It's not just a matter of whether the orchestra and the singers are on key (though that can certainly enhance the worship experience!); it's a matter of knowledge. Not a book knowledge but the knowledge that Paul referred to when he said, "I know whom I have believed" (2 Timothy 1:12 KJV).

One church believes what it is singing, while the other actually knows the Lord and sings about that experience. To realize the power of God in our lives and in our churches, we must move from believing to knowing. Knowing whom you are singing about and praying to puts fire in your worship and passion in your prayer.

Think of the difference of these two statements: I believe in Jesus. I know Jesus.

I am not trivializing the power of the first statement, for certainly that is the foundation of our relationship with God. But to grow in knowledge is to build on the foundation of faith.

In this sense, knowledge is power. Not self-power but power through Christ.

Lord, I want to do more than know about you.
I want to know you!

At the Table with God

Jesus was called, and his disciples, to the marriage.
—John 2:2 KJV

Your friend is getting married. At the wedding there is joy, laughter, and plenty of food, but the wine runs out.

A friend of the family, Mary, is there along with her son. You have heard that he is quite knowledgeable, a man of understanding. Mary whispers something to him. He speaks softly to his mother, then stands alone for a moment. He turns to you and asks you to fill six pots with water. It's a strange request, but you do it. Now he asks you to take a cup of it to your cousin, who's serving as emcee at the party. He drinks it and says, "It's the best wine I've ever tasted!"

Mary's son is smiling. He is seated at a table with a few of his friends. You must find out more about this man! You walk over, introduce yourself, sit down, and look into a kind face with eyes that peer into the depths of your soul. His undivided attention is focused on you.

Though he was fully God, Jesus was also a man who smiled, rejoiced, conversed, and celebrated life. And this same Jesus has invited you to sit beside him at his table. He smiles and pulls out a chair beside him. Will you sit by him, talk with him, listen to him—or will you simply watch from afar?

Oh Jesus, I hear you saying, "Come to me," and I answer,
"Lord, thank you for the invitation! Behold your servant.
I am here!"

Life Infinity

This is life eternal, that they might know thee the only true God, and Jesus Christ.—John 17:3 KJV

The concept of the eternal is beyond my comprehension most of the time. I regularly try to stretch my mental faculties to understand that the life of the soul surpasses the life of the body, but words like *infinity, forever,* and *eternity* defy my rational course of reasoning.

One illustration describes eternity like this: "If a bird flew around the world once a year and brushed its wing against the top of the tallest mountain, when the mountain has become level ground, eternity has just begun." The apostle John said eternal life is found in knowing the "only true God, and Jesus Christ" (John 17:3 KJV). No one else can bring us this kind of rich reward. To know him—not just to know about him—is our highest aim as Christians. Certainly, knowing about him is a worthy goal, but it is not life eternal.

Saint Augustine said, "Thou hast made us for thyself, O Lord, and our hearts are restless until they find their rest in thee." That's why real life does not begin for us until we know God by experience and not just by head knowledge.

God has offered us the way out of this limiting and confining rat race. To know God through Jesus Christ is to know the way out! In him is life infinity (see John 1:4).

Lord Jesus, you have set eternity in my heart.
Though I cannot fathom it, I know it is real,
and I want to experience it through intimacy with you.

Weekend Reflections

The kingdom of God has many principles, from the principle of sowing and reaping to the principle of confession and forgiveness. While all of God's principles and laws are important, some are more consequential.

While God wants us to be successful and to supply our needs, his higher purpose is to bring us into a more intimate relationship with him. That's why "the first and greatest commandment" is "Love the Lord your God with all your heart and with all your soul and with all your mind" (Matthew 22:37–38). God is committed to loving us regardless of our success, our popularity, or our spiritual achievements.

Ripples of Reflection

- God's first priority for you—above your ministry success, your reputation, and your prosperity—is your relationship with him. How should this affect your priorities?

- Consider what it takes to really get to know someone. How does this relate to your getting to know God?

- God loves all the world, but Jesus did have an inner circle of friends. Why did Jesus reveal more to them than he did to the rest?

The Aroma of Christ

We are to God the aroma of Christ among those who are being saved.—2 Corinthians 2:15

Have you noticed that when you are around people with a heavy, negative spirit, their pessimism seems to cling to you after they are gone, while others seem to brighten your day and deposit some of their zest for living into your life? Some people can be such fountains of gloom and doom—and then they wonder why no one wants to be around them.

God wants to anoint us with the oil of gladness and the "fragrance of the knowledge of him" (2 Corinthians 2:14) so that everything and everyone we encounter is blessed by the smooth touch of the Holy Spirit. The words we say should minister grace and excellence, not doubt and depravity. We should edify, or build up, the hearer. God's Word tells us, "Let no corrupt communication proceed out of your mouth, but that which is good to the use of edifying, that it may minister grace unto the hearers" (Ephesians 4:29 KJV).

What will you leave with the ones whose lives you touch today? Are your family members, your coworkers, your fellow worshipers, or the strangers you meet going to be better people for having been with you today? Will you bless them with the fragrance of Christ, the grace you have been freely given?

Lord, may the words of my mouth be as a pleasing fragrance to you so that I can minister grace and life to those around me.

The Blessing of Godly Counsel

In every matter of wisdom and understanding. . . , he found them ten times better.—Daniel 1:20

*W*hen Jerusalem was besieged by Nebuchadnezzar, Daniel and his three friends were summoned to the Babylonian king's palace for three years of instruction in "the language and literature of the Babylonians" (Daniel 1:4). The Bible says they were then ten times wiser than the wise men of Babylon!

God's wisdom exceeds the wisdom of man. Though the Babylonian training certainly helped Daniel, he obviously received heavenly wisdom above and beyond his palace training. Likewise, when a problem is consuming our thoughts, it may be beneficial to confide in a trusted friend and pore over the dilemma together. Godly men or women are plugged in to supernatural wisdom and insight, and we do well to avail ourselves of that connection.

How do we know the wisdom we're getting is heavenly? Consider the words of James: "The wisdom that comes from heaven is first of all pure; then peace-loving, considerate, submissive, full of mercy and good fruit, impartial and sincere" (3:17).

Is the wisdom that's being shared with you full of mercy and peace? Is it submitted to Christ's Lordship? If it is, count yourself blessed.

Father, as your Word instructs me, I ask you for wisdom (see James 1:5). I abandon my pride and seek out godly counsel when it is needed.

Ministering to the Heart

I wrote you out of great distress . . . to let you know the depth of my love for you.—2 Corinthians 2:4

The words with which we minister are meaningful only if our motive is love. Truth spoken without love is noisy and bothersome. It is "as sounding brass, or a tinkling cymbal" (1 Corinthians 13:1 KJV). No real ministry takes place; there is no distinct message. Without love our message is cluttered with the clamor of selfish ambition and personal desire. Truth spoken in love, however, is like "apples of gold in settings of silver" (Proverbs 25:11). It goes straight to the heart because the message is clear, unencumbered with the weight of avarice or self-indulgence.

You may say, "I pray, I fast, and I study, but nothing is happening." But do you love? Is it religion, or is it relationship you seek? Is compassion at the core of your service? Love is the missing ingredient. As we cultivate our intimacy with Jesus, his love will be the source of our ministry. It will be the catalyst for the words we speak and the gospel we must share.

Lord, send your Spirit to check my motives, my ambitions. Let it be love that moves me to speak, to minister, to serve.

Beautiful Feet?

How beautiful upon the mountains are the feet of him that bringeth good tidings.—Isaiah 52:7 KJV

Sister Hawks often stopped me in the sanctuary to share how, yet again, God had supplied her needs in the nick of time. "Let me tell you how God answered my prayer," she would begin.

I always carried away from our encounters some good news about the faithfulness of God. I think of Sister Hawks when I read the beautiful passage from Isaiah: "How beautiful upon the mountains are the feet . . ."

I must admit that I have seen very few "beautiful feet" in my lifetime. I mean, why didn't Isaiah talk about a beautiful mouth or beautiful hands! But beautiful feet? Especially feet that cross a mountain to carry a message. I picture rugged, callused, blistered, and swollen feet that ache at the end of the journey. Why did Isaiah describe them as beautiful?

Perhaps he knew that when you are starved for good news and God sends his messenger to you, every part of that letter carrier seems beautiful, even his or her feet!

Sister Hawks's feet were certainly not beautiful. She struggled with diabetes and poor circulation, so her ankles were usually swollen and her toes were discolored. But in heaven's eyes they were as beautiful as the messages of God's faithfulness she brought to me.

Father, with your help I will be one who brings good news, one who proclaims, "God reigns!"

Guard Your Well

Above all else, guard your heart, for it is the wellspring of life.—Proverbs 4:23

Inside each one of us is a well from which we draw our life, our conversation, our hopes, and our dreams. If we would speak life-giving words, we must allow life-giving words to fill our hearts. If we want to nourish our dreams and live in hope, we must fill our well with water from above. We cannot draw from what is not there.

We have all been surprised from time to time when in frustration or anger we speak words that do not bring life but instead hurt feelings or exhibit carnality. Upon examining our lifestyle, we may find that we have been feeding on similar conversation. Or there may be a deeper cause—a root of fear or insecurity that becomes a breeding ground for low self-esteem and negative thoughts. Either way, the words come from the "overflow of the heart."

We must stand guard at the door of our heart. We must protect what goes into our well. Inside is a wealth of good or evil. "A good man's speech reveals the rich treasures within him" (Matthew 12:35 TLB). In the world of finances, most treasure increases in value over time. This is why we must deal with evil treasure swiftly, removing what is impure and holding on to what is lovely, pure, just, and honest.

Father, send the fire of your Holy Spirit to search my well and burn out the impurities until all that remains are the golden riches of your kingdom.

Weekend Reflections

*S*inger Karen Carpenter died of heart failure at age thirty-two after years of self-abuse from the eating disorder anorexia nervosa. What brought on Karen's fatal obsession with her weight? Three little words. It seems a music reviewer had once dubbed her "Richard's chubby sister."

"The tongue has the power of life and death," the Proverbs tell us (18:21). What message are *you* sharing when you speak?

Ripples of Reflection

- Why is it important to choose our words carefully? (see Matthew 12:36–37).

- Words bring life or destruction. Which way do your words balance out?

- Speak a word of praise or say something positive to everyone you meet today, and be aware of how your comment impacts each person.

Out of the Gate and Winning!

This is the day the LORD has made; let us rejoice and be glad in it.—Psalm 118:24

As a boy, David exhibited a winning attitude when he faced Goliath. While the armies of Israel cowered in the shadows, David stepped out boldly and said, "The LORD who delivered me from the paw of the lion and the paw of the bear will deliver me from the hand of this Philistine" (1 Samuel 17:37). His experiences as a young shepherd boy gave him the courage he needed to face Goliath. This same confident attitude caused the apostle Paul to say, "Forgetting what is behind and straining toward what is ahead, I press on toward the goal to win" (Philippians 3:13–14). He did not set out to lose, but to win! His attitude of confidence in Christ carried him forward.

Do whatever it takes to start your day with the right attitude. Get up on the right side of the bed. Start out on the right foot. Your determination to get started right will go a long way toward making the rest of your day flow smoothly. And just as you start each day with a winning attitude, start your future—right here, right now—with a confident attitude and a sense of God's purpose for your life. Each confident today will lead toward a future of confident tomorrows.

Lord, thank you for renewed courage to face the day.
I will be successful today because you empower me
to triumph over all discouragement.

Living in the Light of the Long Tomorrow

With the Lord a day is like a thousand years, and a thousand years are like a day.—2 Peter 3:8

"When will it be tomorrow?" the little boy asked.

"Tomorrow is the day after today," his mother replied.

"When tomorrow comes, will it still be tomorrow?"

"No. When tomorrow comes, it will be today, and the day after that will be tomorrow."

"I guess it will never be tomorrow, will it?"

Like this little boy, many people seem to have difficulty seeing beyond today. It would be wiser to "think of the long tomorrow," as A. W. Tozer advised.

What would our todays be like if we lived them all in the light of eternity—that "long tomorrow" Tozer mentioned? If we made every decision today based on the weight of eternity, what would our lives look like? How would we spend our time and our money? Would our prized possessions still hold their same attraction?

If you live to be eighty, you will have lived 29,220 days. If you're thirty-five now, you only have about 16,435 days left. Then the long tomorrow begins. Where will you spend forever? The little boy decided that tomorrow never comes, but if you think about it, tomorrow has already begun.

Father, I pray as your servant Moses did, "Teach us to number our days, that we may gain a heart of wisdom"
(Psalm 90:12 NKJV).

Lift Up Your Voice

When he came near the place where the road goes down the Mount of Olives, the whole crowd of disciples began joyfully to praise God in loud voices for all the miracles they had seen.
—*Luke 19:37*

What kind of passion do you put into your prayers? Do you enthusiastically praise God for your blessings? Or do you wait until the last moments of the day, mumble a few words from the Lord's Prayer, then fall asleep?

One way to improve our prayer time is to raise our voices and speak our thoughts out loud. The Gospel of Luke reports that when Jesus entered Jerusalem riding on a colt, the people joyfully praised God in "loud voices." The religious Pharisees told Jesus to rebuke the people, but Jesus refused. He replied, "If they keep quiet, the stones will cry out" (Luke 19:40).

In John's vision of angels worshiping around the throne, he described them as singing in a loud voice (see Revelation 5:11–12). In fact, there are more than a dozen references to loud voices in John's vision—and only one reference to silence.

There is certainly a time when we should be quiet in solemn worship. But there is also a time when it's appropriate to lift our voices to God in prayer and praise. So go ahead. Raise your voice; show your passion for God. Join the worshiper David and sing, "Awake, my soul! Awake, harp and lyre! I will awaken the dawn" (Psalm 57:8).

Lord, I will lift my voice in praise to you.
I love to call on your name. I love to worship you.
With my whole heart I will bless your name.

God Sent You a Gift Today

God again set a certain day, calling it Today.—Hebrews 4:7

I have a closet I've been wanting to clean out for years. I'll bet you have one too—a closet filled with the remnants of good intentions. Maybe you have a stationary bike in there along with a dusty tennis racket, a rusty fishing reel, and a book you never read. There may be brochures for the cruise you never took, postcards you never mailed, and the baseball mitt you bought so you and your kids could play catch. We buy such things with high hopes and vivid dreams. But we wait too long for the circumstances to be just right to carry out our plans. We save the good dishes for special occasions, the skates for a day when the weather is perfect, the Bible study for a time when we aren't quite so busy. We save our good intentions, storing them away in a closet of our house or a corner of our minds, and as a result, words go unsaid, prayers go unprayed, and loved ones pass through our lives not knowing how we feel about them.

God has given us this moment to live, to breathe, to love. We are not promised tomorrow, and we can't hold on to yesterday. What God offers us is a gift: it's called Today.

Father, thank you for this gift of Today. Open my eyes to see the things in it that are most important.

Your Today Impacts Your Tomorrow

Go to the ant, you lazybones; consider its ways, and be wise.
—Proverbs 6:6 NRSV

At one time or another, we've all thought, *I just don't feel like praying. I don't feel like reading the Bible.* When such feelings occur, we're caught in a struggle between the physical and the spiritual. We know what we should do, but somehow we just can't muster the energy or enthusiasm to do it.

What we do in spite of such feelings shows our maturity. Think of the child who says, "I don't feel like going to school today." Let's face it. If most of us had gone to school only when we felt like it, the teacher would have never learned our names! Part of growing up is learning that we will be rewarded later for doing today what we don't really feel like doing. We learn that if we go to school today, we can be more selective in our vocational pursuits later. We learn that if we skip football practice today, we pay a price on game day.

The same is true when it comes to prayer and praise. Even when you don't feel like it, pray! Lay aside the temporary feelings, and fix your eyes on the goal. Keep on studying God's Word. The rewards *will* come.

Lord Jesus, I will not live by how I feel but by my faith. I am not a captive to my emotions; you have freed me to do your will, oh God.

Weekend Reflections

$\mathcal{W}$e cannot change the past.... We cannot change the fact that people will act in a certain way. We cannot change the inevitable. The only thing we can do is play on the string we have, and that is our attitude.... I am convinced that life is 10 percent what happens to me and 90 percent how I react to it" (Charles Swindoll, *Strengthening Your Grip*).

On what "string" are you playing the music of your life? How are you reacting to the things that happen to you? Attitude makes a difference!

Ripples of Reflection

- Think of two incidents that happened in the last week where attitude had a great impact on your relationship with someone.

- Thinking of "the long tomorrow," as A. W. Tozer recommended, what things will you do differently today? How can your attitude affect the conflicts and decisions you are facing?

- Zig Ziglar says that the first greeting you have in the morning is the most important one of the day. What can you do to start the day with a better attitude—and help others to do the same?

The Wings of the Wind

The wind blows wherever it pleases. . . . So it is with everyone born of the Spirit.—John 3:8

Who knows how the wind will blow today? Weather experts take a look at satellite images and atmospheric data and give their educated predictions, but at any time the wind may shift directions unexpectedly. It "blows wherever it pleases." So it is with the Spirit.

The apostle Paul rode the wind of the Holy Spirit as it initiated his first missionary journey and directed him along the way, moving him constantly forward. When the change in the wind came, Paul changed with it. Scripture says, "They tried to enter Bithynia, but the Spirit of Jesus would not allow them to" (Acts 16:7).

God is sovereign. He alone decides where and when the Spirit will blow. We can't control the wind of the Spirit, but we can fly on his wings. God sets the course of the wind of the Spirit. We can't change his direction or slow it down, and we shouldn't try to. Instead, our responsibility is to raise our sails, batten down the hatches if we must, and prepare ourselves for the ride of our lives as we carry God's Word to the world.

Come, Holy Spirit. I give you full authority in my life to lead, direct, and empower me as you will. Oh, that I may be sensitive to your every bidding!

Are You a Kindler?

Do not put out the Spirit's fire.—1 Thessalonians 5:19

God wants his fire to burn in our hearts, cleansing and purging us of everything that is not like Christ and igniting a fire in those around us. This won't happen unless we let his truth blaze within us. As Phillip Brooks said, "Nothing but the fire kindles fire."

I was a firsthand witness to this phenomenon when I was a child. I ran an errand for Mom on my bicycle and was returning home when an electric line about three hundred yards away from me suddenly snapped loose from the pole and began flailing about wildly. Sparks from the broken wire ignited some dry brush, which ignited a nearby pine tree that was loaded with sticky sap. I watched in disbelief as one whole tree after another burst into flames from the bottom up and was completely consumed by flames in a matter of seconds. One tree, afire, kindled the next one.

As Christians we can either ignite God's fire in one another—or we can put it out. We are either fire kindlers or fire quenchers. We're either fanning the flames or we're dousing the live embers of those around us. You can quench the fire, or you can stir it up. Our goal should be "to fan into flame the gift of God" (2 Timothy 1:6).

Lord, I want to keep your fire burning in my heart and in the heart of everyone I know.

By Him, through Him, and in Him

He is before all things, and in him all things hold together.
—Colossians 1:17

As Christians, we see ourselves as channels of God's life and love. We set about doing his work with one hand in God's hand and the other free to minister to others. His beauty and goodness continue to flow through us as long as we stay "plugged in" to the Source.

There is a danger, though, for those who minister, or for those who are creative. If we're not careful, we may come to believe we are ministering out of ourselves. Paul knew this danger. He wrote, "Not that we are competent in ourselves to claim anything for ourselves, but our competence comes from God" (2 Corinthians 3:5). When we start believing we're "competent in ourselves," our focus turns toward the blessing and away from the Blesser. This path, if continually pursued, eventually inhibits the flow of creativity and life.

God has a way of pulling the rug out from under us when we begin to revel in the glory of our gifts, not because he desires to make fools of us, but because he wants to be our sufficiency. He wants us always to need him, to wholly trust and rely on his power within us that he may be glorified in our need. And he wants to flow through us to become a blessing to others.

Father, I recognize my insufficiencies, my needs; I look to you for help. I know that everything I am comes from you.

Becoming Yes-People

The Spirit and the bride say, Come. And let him that heareth say, Come.—Revelation 22:17 KJV

A family, friendship, or church can be stifled by one person with a "no" attitude. This is the person who, when something new is introduced, quickly responds, "But we've never done it that way before!" or who immediately answers, "I can't," when asked to do something that might stretch him or her socially, physically, or spiritually.

There have always been no-people standing ready to shoot down anything new. When Jesus longed to reveal himself to his own extended Jewish family, to demonstrate God's power among them for their own good, most of them shook their heads and argued, "No, he can't be the Messiah. Isn't that the son of the carpenter? Isn't he from Nazareth?" (see Matthew 13:54–56).

Ah, but look what happened to those who said yes.

The gospel of Jesus Christ is a message for the yes-people of the world. Though God has the power to show up whether or not he is welcome, he chooses to reveal himself to those who invite him in. He longs to flow in power and might throughout the earth, but he chooses to enter by standing at the door of our hearts and knocking.

God, I choose to say yes. I want to participate in your kingdom purposes. I want to know you and join you in the field.

Are Your Heart Eyes Open?

I pray also that the eyes of your heart may be enlightened.
—Ephesians 1:18

*H*ow many times have you stood looking right at something but were unable to see it? The working of the Spirit is often like that. Sometimes God is trying to show us something, and the lesson is so obvious we can't see it. As the saying goes, "We can't see the forest for the trees!" Many times we're blinded by our own personal agendas or our preconceived ideas. We're looking for one thing while God is trying to show us another. Or we're misinterpreting the signs all around us.

When we're overlooking the obvious, it may be that we're looking for spiritual things that the carnal mind simply cannot comprehend. This is why God gave us heart eyes, the ability to sense what the natural eyes can't see. Paul explained this ability when he wrote, "'No eye has seen, no ear has heard, no mind has conceived what God has prepared for those who love him'—but God has revealed it to us by his Spirit" (1 Corinthians 2:9–10).

The psalmist asked God to "open my eyes that I may see wonderful things in your law" (Psalm 119:18). We, too, must ask God to open not only our physical eyes but our heart eyes so that we are aware of all the blessings and lessons he has for us.

Lord, give me the eyes of the Spirit to walk circumspectly.
Don't let me overlook the obvious
while searching for some hidden meaning.

Weekend Reflections

The Bible reminds us, "As he is, so are we in this world" (1 John 4:17 KJV). The Holy Spirit gives us the power to live as Christ in this world. We must rely on the Holy Spirit to live holy. Andrew Murray made this principle clear when he said, "A man cannot live one hour of a godly life unless by the power of the Holy Spirit. He may live a proper, consistent life, an irreproachable life, a life of virtue and diligent service. But to live a life acceptable to God in the enjoyment of God's salvation and God's love, to live and walk in the power of the new life—he cannot do it unless he is guided by the Holy Spirit every day and hour" (*Absolute Surrender*).

Ripples of Reflection

- The Holy Spirit guides us into all truth (see John 16:13). How is *guiding* different from *leading*?

- It is the Spirit of God who reveals the thoughts of God (see 1 Corinthians 2:9–11). Are you listening to your own mind (natural reasoning) or to the Spirit? How does listening to the Spirit change your behavior and thoughts?

- Who is the Holy Spirit telling you to pray for this week?

Where There's a Will, There's a Way

The one who calls you is faithful and he will do it.
—*1 Thessalonians 5:24*

*S*ometimes as believers we find ourselves facing a new challenge we feel unprepared for. As God opens the door for a new assignment, we hesitate to abandon the security we have grown accustomed to in order to reach for the unknown. However, God's perfect will for us is always the safest, securest place to be. When we disobey him, we distance ourselves from the protection of his keeping.

For every challenge we face that is truly God-directed, there will be sufficient strength to accomplish the goal. God makes provision for his purpose; he has the best training school imaginable.

Consider how God prepared Moses for the tasks ahead of him by dropping him into the house of Pharaoh, where he received the most elite teaching of his day. Or think of Paul, who studied under the capable teaching of Gamaliel. Neither man knew he was being prepared for a specific calling and purpose that would be presented at a later time. But when God laid out the challenge before these men, their training for the work became obvious.

Is God revealing some new opportunity to you? Do you fear what you have never tried? Don't hesitate! He has equipped you for this moment.

Lord, give me courage to meet the challenges you have set before me and the confidence to know that you have prepared me for such a time as this.

The Living Way

Having therefore, brethren, boldness to enter . . . through the veil,
that is to say, his flesh . . . let us draw near.
—Hebrews 10:19–22 KJV

When we stand at the foot of the cross, we may feel like the children of Israel must have felt as they stood before the curtain in the temple that separated them from the Holy Place. On the other side of that veil was the awesomeness of God, which stood in stark contrast to their own human frailty. And on the other side of the cross of Christ is life with Christ, which is a far cry from the dead life we live without Christ. But in order to share that glorious new life with the Father, we must follow the Son through the veil of death.

When we are faced with the holiness of his glory, we see ourselves in a new light and recognize that part of us must die. So we go the way that millions have gone before, the way of the cross, to nail that part of us that is not like him to the tree.

Dying to self may seem a lonely process, but we do not make this passage alone. There is One who meets us at death's door. On the other side of the door is true life in Christ. So we do not dread the way of death after all, because he is there. He takes our hands and guides us safely to the other side of the Cross into sweet communion with the Father.

Lord, I am comforted knowing you love me
even as I struggle to put to death my old self
so our relationship is restored to closeness.

Who Is That Standing with You?

If God is for us, who can be against us?—Romans 8:31

Have you ever faced something terrifying when you had no choice but to stand there and take it? When I was about twelve years old, I was going door-to-door with two other boys from my Sunday-school class handing out flyers advertising our church's upcoming revival.

At one house we hopped out of the car, walked to the door, rang the bell, and waited. Suddenly we heard the unwelcome sound of the owner's angry dog. As it came tearing around the corner of the house, my two buddies bolted back to the car. I, too, made a run for it, but being the last one back to the car (and the closest one to the dog), I was the one who fell victim to the attacker. The dog took a nip at my backside. Thankfully, it was not a severe wound. The biggest injury was to my pride for having been deserted.

Eventually we all face an attack of some kind. And much to our dismay, our friends may leave us stranded to face the terror alone. In those times, we must pray for the courage to never back down from doing what we know is right. When we are doing the right thing, God is standing with us. When we seek first to obey, we are joining hands with him. And God always wins.

Oh God, you know the things I am facing today. Thank you for being my friend who sticks closer than any brother or sister.

No Mistaken Identity

I will not forget you!—Isaiah 49:15

I was recently in a local hospital to pray a blessing over Becky, a dear woman in the church, before and after the arrival of her tenth child, a beautiful, healthy baby girl. As Becky and her baby cuddled, Becky suddenly lifted her arm and asked her husband, "Did you check the numbers on our bracelets?"

She was referring to the hospital ID bracelets that match the mothers and their babies. "Yes, honey," her husband replied. He then told me about the security system the hospital used that kept the elevator doors from closing if someone tried to leave with a baby.

As I walked out the doors of the hospital, I was reminded of the words of our heavenly Father: "Can a mother forget the baby at her breast and have no compassion on the child she has borne? Though she may forget, I will not forget you!" (Isaiah 49:15). You see, God has his own security number system. He has numbered the hairs on your head! (see Matthew 10:30). There's no mistaken identity in heaven.

God will never forget us. He knows our names—*and* our numbers.

"How precious to me are your thoughts, O God! . . . Were I to count them, they would outnumber the grains of sand"
(Psalm 139:17–18).

The Life of Ease

The LORD confides in those who fear him; he makes his covenant known to them.—Psalm 25:14

What do you fear? failure? the future? Did you know there is a bypass around this blockade of fear or worry? It is a covenant relationship with our heavenly Father. It is wholly trusting and leaning on the God we worship with reverence and awe. In this kind of relationship, he teaches us to know his ways, which are higher than our ways and beyond human understanding.

As he confides these secrets in us, the covenant relationship develops, our eyes are enlightened, and our spiritual senses are finely tuned to see, to hear, and to know. Writing to the Ephesian church, the apostle Paul prayed "that the eyes of your heart may be enlightened in order that you may know the hope to which he has called you" (Ephesians 1:18).

As we love God and show reverence for him, his ways begin to unfold before us. Soon we have exchanged fear and worry for confidence and trust. Are you ready to trade your anguish and anxiety for peace of mind? Place the Lord at the highest place of reverence in your life, enter into a covenant relationship with him, then listen as he shares his secrets and reveals his ways to you.

Father, help me put everything in my life in proper prospective as I lift you to the highest point of reverence in my life.

Weekend Reflections

It was 1947. As Jackie Robinson, the first African American in Major League Baseball, ran onto the field in Cincinnati, jeers and ridicule bellowed from the stands. But when his team captain and friend, Pee Wee Reese, walked over and put his arm around him, the crowd grew silent. Suddenly, Jackie was no longer alone. Our confidence as believers is based on who's standing beside us. It isn't so much self-confidence as it is God-confidence.

Ripples of Reflection

- What are you facing that causes you to be filled with dread? What would Christ say to you regarding this worry? (see Hebrews 13:6).

- Timidity does not come from God (see 2 Timothy 1:7). Where *does* it come from?

- Boldness comes when you fear God more than you fear man (see Proverb 29:25). Whom do you fear?

Peace in Prison

But while Joseph was there in the prison, the LORD was with him.—Genesis 39:20–21

Ever since his childhood dream foretelling that his brothers would someday bow down to him, Joseph's life had been one tragic event after another, from being sold as a slave by his brothers to being falsely accused by his boss's wife. Now, in prison, he surely had the opportunity to question what God had in mind for him. Yet Joseph remained faithful.

There's something about godly men and women. They rise to the top, no matter where they are. They may be out of the public eye, but they are never out of God's sight.

God kept his hand on Joseph. Before long, he became a powerful official, and his brothers did, indeed, bow down to him, begging for mercy. God never lost sight of another little shepherd boy out on the hills of Judea. No one suspected that this boy, David, would someday be king. But then, no one suspected that the boy who worked in his father's carpenter shop was the Creator of the world around him.

The wonderful truth that arises in all of this is that God knows where we are. We are to expect and enjoy the kindness, favor, and care of our heavenly Father, who sees us no matter where we are.

Lord, regardless of where I am, your eyes are ever on me. I thank you for your kindness, your favor, that you freely give.

The Price of Character

Tribulation produces perseverance: and perseverance, character.
—Romans 5:3–4 NKJV

Do you sometimes find yourself looking at the seemingly good life of others and saying, "Why not me, God? How come they seem to get all the blessing?" What you may not know is the crises they have endured and the storms they have encountered that have brought them to that level. What trials have they faced that have caused their roots to sink deep into the true knowledge of God? How much wisdom have they gained in their pursuit of God? These are the questions that must be asked. Character is built by the way we choose to respond to the hard times and crises.

Jesus said those who "have not been faithful in the unrighteous mammon [money]" cannot be trusted with true spiritual riches (Luke 16:11 KJV). In other words, those who are not good stewards over what they have now, whether it is natural or spiritual, cannot be entrusted with more. Only those who show themselves faithful in the small things will find themselves "trusted with much" (16:10).

As character grows, so grows the capacity to serve. As our relationship with Christ grows, so grows our responsibility in his kingdom. As our ability to follow grows, so grows our ability to lead.

Father, on the other side of the storm, I see a stronger child of God. Oh Lord, give me a heart that trusts you.

A Rich Welcome

God will open wide the gates of heaven for you to enter.
—2 Peter 1:11 NLT

When traveling through airports, my favorite scenes feature travelers who begin craning their necks as they approach baggage claim, eagerly scanning the waiting crowd to find those who are there to meet them. Children are usually the most unrestrained in showing their emotions. They leap into the open arms of a parent or grandparent and allow themselves to be smothered with kisses for a few seconds. Sweethearts, on the other hand, may linger for several moments, locked in an embrace.

I love going home for the holidays and walking through the doorway to find that Mom has the table set and the candles lit. Fresh loaves of pumpkin bread, still warm from the oven, are usually waiting on the counter. Warmth, love, smiles, hugs, and food welcome me; it's a reception anyone would look forward to.

It's wonderful to be welcomed. But even the warmest welcome here on earth cannot compare with the exuberant greeting the Lord himself will extend to us someday. For his faithful servants, God will open wide the pearly gates and say, "You have done well. Welcome to the joy of heaven!" (Matthew 25:21, my paraphrase).

Jesus is now preparing a glorious reception for you. The table is being set, and the heavenly band is warming up.

Lord Jesus, I want to live so that I can hear you say, "Well done, good and faithful servant!" (Matthew 25:21, 23).

"But It Doesn't Look Dead"

These . . . men are . . . clouds without water, . . . autumn trees
without fruit, doubly dead, uprooted.—*Jude 12 NASB*

Jesus was hungry, but when he scanned a fig tree, looking for fruit, it had none. Jesus cursed the tree, and it withered (see Matthew 21:19). One principle revealed in this story is that fruit trees are not planted to just stand there and look good, but to bear fruit. Jesus plainly spoke of this when he said, "By this My Father is glorified, that you bear much fruit; so you will be My disciples" (John 15:8 NKJV).

Jude wrote about some people who apparently were making the rounds, "doing lunch" with various churches. In an effort to promote themselves for selfish gain, they were apparently making great promises. But when it came time to deliver, they produced no fruit.

There is only one Lord of the harvest. Ultimately, how much fruit we bear depends on the one who said, "Without Me you can do nothing" (John 15:5 NKJV).

Beware! Some trees look good, but they bear no fruit. Some people may look the part and even say some of the right things, but inside they are dead. No power, no life, no fruit. "They are like clouds blowing over dry land without giving rain, promising much but producing nothing. They are like trees without fruit at harvesttime" (Jude 12 NLT).

Apart from you, Lord Jesus, I can do nothing.
I will bear no fruit if I do not abide in you.

So You Want to Lead?

At my first defense, no one came to my support, but everyone deserted me.—2 Timothy 4:16

The picture of a man such as Paul standing alone is both inspiring and discouraging. A man who risked his life for others now found no one to stand beside him in the crucial hour of testing. When his life was hanging in the balance, none of his earthly friends were there to comfort him. Still, Paul, a man of character, stood firm for what he believed.

The willingness to stand alone is what being a leader is all about. To lead others is to point the way and do the right thing, even when no one else has enough courage to stand with you. Being a Christian leader means boldly sounding the clarion call that points men and women to the way of holiness when everyone else is calling for compromise.

For the sake of so-called unity, do we allow ourselves to be persuaded to abandon the principles that were forged in us by a praying mother, a God-fearing father, or a faithful teacher? Or do we have the character to stand firm in what we believe?

To do the right thing when it's popular takes excellence. To do the right thing when no one cares takes integrity. But to do the right thing when peers forsake you and others say you're being dogmatic, now that takes character!

Father, lead me in the right way, not the way that "seems" right.
Give me unfailing courage to choose the high way,
not the low path of destruction.

Weekend Reflections

"$\mathcal{D}$ aniel distinguished himself above the governors and satraps, because an excellent spirit was in him; and the king gave thought to setting him over the whole realm" (Daniel 6:3 NKJV). Daniel was in the midst of a godless nation and political structure, yet he kept "an excellent spirit." Since we are representatives of God's heavenly kingdom, we should be committed to excellence, no matter where we find ourselves stationed and no matter that we stand alone except for God.

Ripples of Reflection

- Are you committed to excellence on your job or in your stay-at-home or voluntary role?

- *Excellent* means "extraordinary." It's a mark above the rest. What do you do that is excellent?

- If we are faithful stewards with what God has given, God often gives us more (see Luke 16:10). What evidence do you see of this promise in your own life?

At the Proper Time . . .

Let us not become weary in doing good, for at the proper time we will reap a harvest.—Galatians 6:9

Are you weary of doing good? The work God has called us to will not always be glorious. In fact it can be quite ordinary. Tedious. More like a yoke than a gift. Certainly, there may be glorious times—those Mount of Transfiguration experiences when we want to stop and build a temple. There may even be days when we think we can hear the rushing wind of Pentecost and we're so inspired that we're ready to head off into the mission field. But eventually we have to come down off the mountain and carry on with our everyday activities. The rushing wind moves on, and so must we, back into those narrow, breezeless trenches of ordinariness.

Later, perhaps, we may realize that it was those joyful moments of inspiration that prepared us for the stormy nights when we felt adrift in a sea of trials that otherwise would have drowned our hope, extinguished our zeal, and crippled our weary bodies. Clinging to the lifeline of faith, we wait for God to hear our cries. Then the sun comes up again, and we toil on.

God sees us working . . . sometimes wearily. He knows the seeds we have faithfully sown in earnest prayer, and only he knows when the harvest will come. So we cast off our weariness; we will not give up, knowing our glory lies ahead. It will come at the right time—God's time—not a second early, not a moment too late.

Thank you, Lord, for your faithfulness,
not just to hear my prayers, but to supply
what I really need—when the time is right.

Patience for the Harvest

Jesus grew both tall and wise, and was loved by God and man.—Luke 2:52 TLB

Possibly no other aspect of Jesus's life has been theorized about more than those silent years between ages twelve and thirty. Because the Bible has so little to say about this span of time, we must resist the temptation to surmise or fabricate. It would be wonderful to know more about this period, but because the Bible is silent, we must also remain silent.

The truth that is revealed, however, is that "Jesus grew tall and wise." There had to be time for him to experience life as a child and as a young man . . . to be a boy, then a teenager, so that he might "sympathize with our weaknesses" (Hebrews 4:15). To state it more simply, he had to be a boy before he could be a man.

The growing season can be exasperating. Nothing expends our patience like waiting for the harvest. But in the kingdom of God, there is no instant maturity. We need the Father's patience; no one suffers along with us like he does. And if he is willing to wait, should not we have the same forbearance with ourselves? If we dare to be mighty men and women of God, we must first learn to be his children.

Lord, thank you for your patience, your mercy that endures forever. Let me be content to sit at your feet before I go out to slay giants in my life.

Keep on Doing It!

Do not merely listen to the word, and so deceive yourselves. Do what it says.—James 1:22

It is one thing to hear God's Word but another thing to obey. Are you doing what he has said, or have you merely listened? Obedience isn't always exciting. Sometimes it's downright monotonous. It is then that we must keep our eyes set on the joy awaiting us—the joy of the harvest. The key is to obey.

"But I have," you may say. "I have shared the gospel, and people just reject it."

Even when our message seems ineffective, we must keep on declaring the good news. Only God knows who will receive it. Just because someone rejects it does not mean the Word does not work. Sooner or later, the seed we sow will land on good ground and a bountiful harvest will result. Jesus said, "The seed on good soil stands for those with a noble and good heart, who hear the word, retain it, and by persevering produce a crop" (Luke 8:15).

Pray, and keep on praying. Preach, and keep on preaching. Believe, and keep on believing. You may not see immediate results, but you *will* see results. People did not always receive the apostle Paul's message, but he kept at it because he knew that "at the proper time we will reap a harvest if we do not give up" (Galatians 6:9).

Oh Father, strengthen my tenacity to persevere in doing the right things despite weariness and discouragement. I know the harvest will come.

Hang On to Your Future

The thief comes . . . to steal and kill and destroy; I have come that they may have life . . . to the full.—John 10:10

What vision has God placed in your heart? Has he given you a promise that seems like something impossible to fulfill? If it is a promise from God, it could very likely seem unthinkable in your present circumstances. After all, God enjoys confounding human wisdom, specifically our carnal reasoning.

Even when the promise seems implausible, hold fast to it, stand firm, and keep the dream alive. These are the actions God expects us to take. When he plants a promise in our spirits, he depends on us to believe his word. Be alert to the enemy's trickery. He comes in many disguises to "steal and kill and destroy," and he may try to steal your future by destroying the vision God has planted deep in your spirit.

The book of Hebrews tells us that Moses was able to leave the security of Egypt "by faith . . . not fearing the king's anger; he persevered because he saw him who is invisible" (11:27). Moses had a vision of the invisible. He had faith in God's promises.

Will you take God at his word? Will you believe the vision he has placed in your heart? Hold on to his promise. It is your future and your life.

Father, illuminate my spiritual vision and ignite a holy fire in me so that I remember the word of the Lord and hold on to what you have promised.

He Is the Author and the Finisher of Our Faith

. . . looking unto Jesus the author and finisher of our faith.
—Hebrews 12:2 KJV

It is one thing to understand how God "begins" our faith and still another to comprehend that he also finishes it. It is easy for me to agree that he has initiated my faith but more difficult for me to agree that he is completing it day by day and glory to glory. Such agreement seems to remove me from the picture, as far as my faith is concerned. And there are times when I want to believe that I am saving my own soul.

Only Christ has the power to save me, and he *is* saving me today and tomorrow. I cannot, by sheer willpower, perfect the image of Jesus Christ in me. Only as I allow his grace to work in my life can the nature of Christ be revealed in me.

It seems that it is only when I am totally helpless, realizing my powerlessness the same way the apostle Paul described in Romans 7, that I am truly aware and totally dependent on Christ in me. Paul talked about the futility of trying to do good apart from Christ and ended by saying, "What a wretched man I am! Who will rescue me from this body of death? Thanks be to God—through Jesus Christ our Lord!" (Romans 7:24–25).

Lord, I realize that apart from you, I am powerless.
But with you nothing is impossible, and that includes becoming
more like you.

Weekend Reflections

*T*here's only one recipe for patience: tough times. As James said, "The testing of your faith produces patience" (1:3 NKJV). Patience is a virtue that is developed in us, not zapped into us. As it grows, it produces a faith that trusts in God and waits for his timing. As Oswald Chambers said, "There are times when you cannot understand why you cannot do what you want to do. When God brings the blank space, see that you do not fill it in, but wait" (*My Utmost for His Highest*).

Ripples of Reflection

- Think of some times when your impatience has caused you to miss out on the ideal.

- Do you know someone who exhibits patience? What results does patience bring this person?

- Looking back, think of how God has developed patience in you.

Temptation Meets Opportunity

She called a man to shave off the seven braids of his hair. . . .
And his strength left him.—Judges 16:19

Why couldn't Samson figure out the evil scheme Delilah was up to? After the first time he fell asleep and she bound him up, it should have been obvious. But this is what happens when we place ourselves in "the lap" of temptation. Our spiritual senses become overwhelmed by the lure of what is desirable to the carnal nature.

This story illustrates the two factors that are involved in committing sin: temptation and opportunity. Despite our best intentions, they will meet from time to time, but there are precautionary measures we can take to reduce the likelihood of that happening. If only Samson had taken these steps! What a difference it would have made!

We must identify the situations and times when we are most vulnerable to temptation and learn how to avoid them. In these situations we're vulnerable to the sin that "easily entangles" us (Hebrews 12:1).

We must take responsibility to keep ourselves as far away as we can get from people, places, and things that can create easy opportunities for us to sin. As the apostle Paul instructed us, "Each of you should learn to control his own body" (1 Thessalonians 4:4). This means if you're a Samson, don't lay your head in Delilah's lap!

Shepherd of my soul, you know my ways, my thoughts. Lead me in the way of truth, in your paths, away from temptation.

Here and Now

Surely I am with you always, to the very end of the age.
—Matthew 28:20

One of the tragedies of modern religion is that it seems to remove God from the personal. Instead of close communion between God and mankind, religion becomes a detached fellowship separated by ritual and formality.

We can learn some important lessons by studying Jesus's interactions with the religious leaders of his day. It might be surprising to realize that he spoke more harshly to them than to any other group—largely because they sought to elevate themselves above the common people he came to seek and to save. The Pharisees and other religious leaders could not see that he had come to build a bridge between God and humankind, to bring God close to his people and establish close communion with them.

Even today it's easy for the erroneous concept of a God far removed to sneak into our thinking. We seem so insignificant in light of the universe and all that is in it. Why would the Creator of the world want to be close to us?

Because he loves us! And he wants to stay close to us. He has inscribed our names on his hands (see Isaiah 49:16). He shelters us in the shadow of his wings (see Psalm 17:8), and nothing can separate us from his love (see Romans 8:38–39).

Holy God, I worship you because you are awesome,
but I am thankful that you are closer than a brother
(see Proverbs 18:24).

That Happened to You Too?

No temptation has seized you except what is common to man.
—*1 Corinthians 10:13*

*I*t wasn't too many weeks after I was born again that I was plagued with doubts about my experience. *Maybe I'm not really saved. What if this whole thing is fake?* I worried. My questions and self-doubt grew until it consumed my spiritual life. I couldn't sing with confidence. I couldn't pray. *After all*, I figured, *what's the use if I'm not really saved?*

Then during one Sunday-evening service, a woman who had served the Lord many years gave a short testimony. I was both shocked and relieved to hear her say, "You know what the devil told me today? He told me I wasn't saved! Now here I am, forty years after being saved, and he tries to tell me that. Can you believe it?"

Her words were like music to my ears. I suddenly realized that the doubt I had felt was actually the enemy of my soul feeding me lies. If someone could know the Lord as long as that sister of the faith had known him and still be tempted to doubt, then I would worry no more about my own bouts of questioning.

Getting a glimpse of another Christian's trial of faith gives us confidence to know that we are not alone in our troubles. And as we hear another's testimony of overcoming, we, too, vow to overcome!

> *Lord Jesus, I will not fear, because you have overcome and your overcoming power is alive in me.*

Winning Is Everything

Our struggle is not against flesh and blood.—Ephesians 6:12

As you gingerly make your way through the morning traffic, you are minding your own business when a little red sports car moves up behind you. You are keeping a safe distance between you and the car in front of you, but Little Red tails you like you're the only thing between him and a wild ride on the autobahn. If you have to stop suddenly, Little Red will be in your front seat.

Thoughts come unbidden into your head: I think I'll just tap my brakes and send Little Red a message, or, I'll get in the next lane and match the speed of the car in front of him and block his path. Maybe that will teach Little Red a little lesson!

In the case of you versus Little Red, who is the most dangerous enemy? Is it Little Red? Or is it Satan working through your stinking pride? By recognizing the real enemy, you can come out on top and win the most important battle: the spiritual battle for your soul.

Use your spiritual energy to put the enemy where he belongs: under your feet, not in a cloud of smoke from your tailpipe! Remember, the enemy doesn't show up in a red suit with a pitchfork. Sometimes he shows up in your mirror.

Lord, give me the insight to discern the real enemy,
to walk and live as a free child of God,
not as a person enslaved to my old nature.

Jesus, Our Helper

He himself [in His humanity] has suffered in being tempted
(tested and tried).—Hebrews 2:18 AMP

As believers, temptations come to us that bring mental pain as well as physical suffering. How many times have we wondered, *How can I be a Christian and be tempted in such a way?* This kind of suffering can be worse than physical suffering because it can destroy our relationship with Christ. We want to please him, to be loved and accepted by him, and this kind of suffering can destroy our security and confidence in Christ.

Jesus knew such trials would beset us. He knew because he endured them himself. He lived as a man and "was in all points tempted as we are" (Hebrews 4:15 NKJV). Not only did he experience temptation, but he also endured the suffering that is a part of it. That's why he sent the Helper to be with us in our hour of temptation.

We are never alone in this struggle. Jesus is with us in our trials and in our suffering. No matter how bad the situation gets, the only direction Jesus runs is toward his children . . . to help us, to relieve us, to aid us. Never will he forsake us. Never will he run the other way.

Lord Jesus, you know my weaknesses and see me in my darkest hour. I lift up my suffering to you with a thankful heart.

Weekend Reflections

*S*in is never satisfied. Giving in to temptation only means there will be a greater desire next time, a deeper chasm longing to be filled. Sinful desire is a bottomless pit, a black hole.

Ask Solomon. In his desire to find the goodness of life, he said, "I denied myself nothing my eyes desired; I refused my heart no pleasure.... Yet when I surveyed all that my hands had done ..., everything was meaningless" (Ecclesiastes 2:10–11).

There is only one who can fill the chasm. The next time you are tempted to sin, listen. See if you don't hear the voice of God saying, "Turn to me instead." When we are tempted, we have a choice: we can turn to what is meaningless, or we can turn to God.

Ripples of Reflection

- What things have you pursued only to find them meaningless?

- In the things we desire most, we can often see the aspect that is lacking in our relationship with God. Considering this possibility, what hunger in your soul do you need God to fill?

- In the hour of your temptation, how can you turn to Jesus in a practical way?

Does Time Fly?

One day is with the Lord as a thousand years, and a thousand years as one day.—2 Peter 3:8 KJV

We all have those days when we look at the clock and it's 2:00 p.m., and then we look at the clock three hours later and it's 2:05. On the other hand, we've also experienced those days when the hours seem to vaporize. How we perceive time's passing depends on whether we're doing something we enjoy or something we dread.

The psalmist said that one day in God's presence is better than a thousand days spent elsewhere (see 84:10). While most scholars agree that 2 Peter 3:8 refers to our life in eternity, I believe the verse offers a lesson for today as well. When we get beyond the thees and thous and arrive at that place of intimate fellowship with God, we should agree with the psalmist that our time spent with the Lord should be a time of joy and blessing. If our time seems to drag by when we're in prayer—if one day seems to drag by as if it were a thousand years—we need to re-examine our relationship. Maybe we're in prayer instead of in his presence. Maybe we're in church instead of in Christ. "This is life eternal," Jesus said, to "know . . . God" (see John 17:3 KJV).

Father, I come into your presence with praise and adulation, treasuring the time I spend worshiping at your feet.

To Open, to Hear, to Know

If any man hear my voice, and open the door,
I will come in.—Revelation 3:20 KJV

What a picture this text creates! It does not take a great imagination to envision the scene. Often used in sermons of evangelism, this passage reaches out to those who have never met the Lord. But I believe the context of this verse shows that it applies even more directly to believers than to nonbelievers.

Jesus does not force his way in. We must open the door. Perhaps we've even invited him to come into our lives. But we have to do more than give lip service. We have to take action, opening the door of our heart and allowing him to enter.

Also, we must be in a position to hear Jesus's voice, because that is what draws us into relationship with him. Certainly, as believers we often find ourselves in situations where his Word—his voice—is shared. We must learn to recognize that voice in our hearts and humbly listen to him.

Jesus stands at the door of our hearts. Have you heard his voice today? Will you open yourself to him and seek his fellowship as he seeks yours?

Keep knocking on my door, Lord. Put me in the position to hear your voice. Keep calling me into a deeper relationship with you.

Come Home!

Thou wilt keep him in perfect peace, whose mind is stayed on thee.—Isaiah 26:3 KJV

*I*f you have ever traveled for any length of time, you know the truth of the old cliché "There's no place like home." There you can relax in your chair, sleep in your bed, and cook what you want in your own kitchen. At home you can be truly at ease, comfortable to just be yourself. There's no one to impress, no one to feign sincerity to.

In the beginning, God made a home for his creation. There, in the Garden, Adam and Eve were in perfect harmony with each other and with God. Naked, they felt no shame because there was nothing to hide from God. Then sin entered the picture, and they were driven out of the beautiful, peaceful garden God had prepared for them. Now there was no rest. No home.

We would all be "homeless" still, except that Jesus came to build a road so we could find our way home. Today the only home for our hearts is in his presence. Just as we weary travelers can never really rest until we are in our own physical homes, so our spirits cannot rest until we are in his blessed presence.

Are you tired of traveling? Go home, where you long to be. Is your spirit weary? Come home to his presence. There you will find peace.

Father, I want to be where you are, for your presence is home. Thank you for your mercy, which endures forever.

A Solitary Place

*Jesus got up, left the house and went off to a solitary place,
where he prayed.—Mark 1:35*

Throughout the centuries God has called those who will
listen to solitary places. It was while he was tending his sheep,
alone on the far side of the desert, that Moses met God in
the burning bush. John was in exile on the tiny isle of Patmos
when he had the brilliant vision of the glorified Christ.

Maybe there are times when God tries to get through to
us amid the clamor and hubbub of our busy lives, but we can't
see or hear him. Then, suddenly, our jobs call us to a lonely
place far from family and friends where we feel forsaken
and long for a familiar face. Or perhaps in difficult times we
find ourselves lost in a spiritual wilderness, wondering where
God is. It may be that these feelings are no accident.

Have you been secretly crying out for renewal and a fresh
revelation of Christ in your life? Maybe he has led you to this
place to answer your prayer. Maybe this is where your heart
can be quiet and you will hear his voice.

Jesus knew where to find strength. He knew how to
commune with his Father. He "went off to a solitary place."
Are you looking for him? He may be waiting for you there,
in that solitary place.

*Lord, I thank you for using the lonely places in my life. There is
nowhere so far away that you do not know where I am.*

Sabbath of the Soul

He said to them, "The Sabbath was made for man, not man for the Sabbath."—Mark 2:27

Sometimes we forget that God's laws are meant to protect us, not to restrict us. Jesus's statement regarding the Sabbath answered a question the religious people asked after Jesus had healed a man. Jesus made it clear that God did not create the law of the Sabbath and then create man so he would have somebody to obey that law. God gave us the Sabbath because he knew we needed it! When we break the Sabbath, we hurt ourselves more than we hurt God.

We are "fearfully and wonderfully made," the psalmist said (139:14), and as complex creatures, we need rest for the spirit, soul, and body. If we do not get enough rest, our bodies may go on strike, and soon we find ourselves resting whether or not we want to!

It is much the same in our souls. They, too, need time to recuperate. I believe this is why our emotions run in waves and why, sometimes, after an emotional high we suddenly find ourselves on an emotional low. Our souls need time to rest, and God has ways of bringing us to rest, even when we do not think we need it: "He makes me lie down in green pastures, he leads me beside quiet waters, he restores my soul" (Psalm 23:2–3).

Jesus, you are Lord of the Sabbath. When you bid me to come to you and rest, I know I will find rest for my soul.

Weekend Reflections

God made a home for our spirits: the presence of God. Ever since Adam and Eve were removed from the place where they walked and talked with God (see Genesis 3), humankind has been in search of this home. As believers we have the privilege of living in God's presence. Whether we are at school, in the car, or on the job, we can still be at home in Christ.

Ripples of Reflection

- Brother Lawrence believed that "all spiritual life consists of practicing God's presence" (*The Practice of the Presence of God*). Contemplate how you can practice the presence of God.

- Adam and Eve hid from God's presence. Do you hide from his presence? If so, why?

- The psalmist wrote that in his presence is "fullness of joy" (16:11 NKJV). What does this phrase mean to you?

You Are Not Your Own

Ye are bought with a price.—1 Corinthians 6:20 KJV

It is an imaginary scene—and yet it is real: the auctioneer in his gibberish shouts out the bids, and slavemasters peer at the slave with discriminating eyes, wanting the most for their money. The slave, standing alone, shudders as someone shouts out a bid. She knows that one. He is known for his intolerance and his abuse. "Going once . . . going twice . . ."

Then, just before the dreaded cry "Sold!" seals her fate, a strong voice shouts out a bid from the back of the crowd, and the other slavemasters gasp. No one has ever paid that much for a slave!

Hurriedly the stranger steps up to claim his newest possession. He helps her from the auction block, removes her shackles, looks into her eyes, and says, "Go free."

I cannot begin to imagine the horror of actually standing on an auction block. Yet, as Christians, this is our story. We were enslaved to serve the master of sin, who abused us by his evil devices. There, in our weakness and bondage, we waited. Then Christ came. He paid the highest price one could pay.

Is it any wonder why we should serve him with our very lives? He loved us and bought us when no one else could see our worth.

Father, once we were slaves to a master we could not escape
from. But you have set us free!

Do You Want to Let It Go?

Jesus . . . asked him, "Do you want to get well?"—John 5:6

When Jesus walked the earth, it was common to see many sick people and beggars lying beside the roadways. Undoubtedly, some of them found the begging lifestyle to be quite profitable, and they had no real desire to change even when the opportunity arose. Perhaps that is why Jesus asked this man beside the pool at Bethesda, "Do you want to get well?"

This story always reminds me of children who pout when they don't get their way. No matter what anybody does or says, the child refuses to smile, laugh, or enjoy whatever might be going on around him or her. Some of us never outgrow this grudge-holding tendency. As adults many of us still hold on to our anger and refuse to forgive our offenders, even to the point of becoming ill. The sad thing about this is that God does not help us get well until we decide to let go of our anger. He waits for us to say, "I want to be happy. I want to forgive. I want to be well."

Do you want to get well? Do you want to be happy? Are you willing to let your anger go? Will you choose now to forgive? These are the questions you must ask yourself before God can heal you.

Lord, I want to get well! Help me release the anger
that impoverishes my spirit. I choose to forgive
and move on in your love.

Grace for You and from You

With the measure you use, it will be measured to you.
—Luke 6:38

"Sow, and you will reap; give, and you will receive" isn't just a principle of finance but of life.

Are you a generous giver, willing to share the blessings God has given you? If so, you probably find most of the people around you to be generous in return. But this biblical principle doesn't apply only to material goods. It also pertains to giving of ourselves, of our knowledge, our devotion, our love. Jesus went out among the people to share the good news. So should we. If we isolate ourselves, tending only to our own needs, how can we follow his example?

And there's something else this principle teaches, something that may be the most difficult lesson of all. It tells us to forgive so that we will be forgiven.

It is in administering grace and forgiveness to others that we find grace for ourselves. Even when they don't deserve it, even when they don't ask for it, we forgive them, because in doing so, we learn about the free gift of grace, which God applies so generously to our own failures and weaknesses.

Be merciful. Do not judge or condemn. Forgive others. Give generously. And be filled.

Lord, I want to be a person who pours grace on others. Because
I am forgiven, I forgive. Because I have received so much,
I will be a giver.

Free Indeed!

*A slave has no permanent place in the family, but a son belongs
to it forever. So if the Son sets you free, you will be free
indeed.—John 8:35–36*

A slave cannot free another slave. The power to set a
slave free is reserved for the slavemaster or a higher authority.
Jesus was not a slave but a Son. He was the Creator of all of
us who, through Adam, were born slaves to sin. But though
we were born slaves to sin, we don't have to remain enslaved
to its power. We were created in the image of God as God's
property, but we have the power to choose our master. When
we choose Jesus, he sets us free and makes us "free indeed"!

Only Jesus has the authority to declare you free. He said,
"All authority in heaven and on earth has been given to me"
(Matthew 28:18). As long as you serve sin, you remain a
slave to its power over you. But once you choose Jesus as
your Savior and Lord, you are free to serve him. You are no
longer a slave but a son—a joint heir with Jesus Christ to all
that the Father freely gives!

*Jesus, thank you for setting me free to serve you and to leave the
slavery of sin. Sin is no longer my master.*

I Am Not Who I Was

To each kind of seed he gives its own body.
—*1 Corinthians 15:38*

The simple truth of being born again can be summed up like this: We die to who we are and rise from death to live as new creations through faith in the power of Jesus Christ. We are not reformed; we are reborn. We lose our old identities and find new ones in Christ Jesus.

The new creatures we become are nothing like our old selves. Our old natures were the seeds, the shells, that died in the ground so our new creations could spring to life. Seeds do not have the same form as the plant; the acorn is not the oak tree. The seed looks nothing like the tree. But when it is planted in the ground and dies, up springs a mighty, living thing that bears no resemblance to the seed!

In the same way, we, as new creations in Christ, do not resemble our old natures. We live not in the seed that was but out of a new creation that exists by the resurrection power of Jesus Christ.

Don't be bound by who you were. That old creature has no relevance to who you are now. That was the seed that died so the new creature could spring to life. You are a new person with a proud heritage and a rich inheritance!

Father, thank you that I am not who I was. You have made me a brand-new being. I have faith in your ability to cause me to live as a new creation.

Weekend Reflections

*Y*ou can't know what freedom means until you've experienced it. You can hear about it and talk about it, but freedom is best understood by living it. You especially appreciate freedom when you know how much it costs. Jesus didn't pour out his life for us so we could be half free. Instead, we "were called to be free" (Galatians 5:13)—"free indeed"! (John 8:36).

Ripples of Reflection

- Are you living free? Why or why not?

- Walking back into sin is like walking back into prison. What are the similarities?

- How can you best preach freedom to those imprisoned by Satan and self?

Do You Know Who You Are?

Now we are children of God.—1 John 3:2

*E*veryone struggles with insecurity at some level. While some people deal with it as a minor issue, others are held captive by its grip. They fear new situations so greatly that they are immobilized, unable to accomplish what is within their reach. On the other hand, confident individuals face new situations with hope and excitement about the adventure and challenge.

If you're a confident person, secure in your God-given abilities, you've been given the gift of affirmation somewhere in your lifetime. You know who you are, and you feel comfortable with that knowledge. You don't fear rejection because you know that how another might see you does not change your personal worth.

As confident Christians, secure in the promise that God loves and cherishes us, we come eagerly before the Lord, knowing he delights in our devotion. We recognize who we are: chosen and beloved children created by a holy God, not because of our merit, not because we've earned a prize or joined an exclusive club, but by the grace of God. Being God's child is a gift, one that empowers us to confidently claim the authority we have as believers, and face whatever lies ahead with courage and faith.

Father, thank you for choosing me even before the foundation of the world. Today I am a child of God, a joint heir with Christ.

Gene Therapy

Ye must be born again.—John 3:7 KJV

Most psychologists agree that we are predisposed to be outgoing, shy, bold, or sociable according to the traits that have been passed on to us, and they say that most of our personality is formed by the age of five. While our environment can affect our personality, *most* of who we are, they say, is "written in our genes."

It's a common thing these days to hear people use their genetic makeup as some sort of excuse. They say, "I can't help it. It's just the way I am."

Our personality is "born of the flesh." That is why we must be born again "of the Spirit," as Jesus said. If we are going to manifest the love, patience, and goodness of Christ, we are going to need a new nature. The hope for us and for everyone who believes is that when we are born again, we acquire a bent toward godliness instead of toward sin. It's as if God has infused our spiritual DNA with the power of the resurrected Christ! (see Galatians 2:20). Now when we're asked how we can love when there is reason to hate, to forgive instead of holding a grudge, and to pray for our enemies instead of seeking revenge, we can say, "I can't help it. It's written in my genes."

Father, I thank you that the same Spirit that raised Jesus from the dead is living in me. I am obligated to sin no longer.

When Was the Last Time You Built an Altar?

He erected there an altar, and called it Elelohe-Israel.
—Genesis 33:20 KJV

The literal meaning of the word *altar* is "slaughter place." Not a pretty image, is it? To many people the church altar has become merely a place where we pay our respects to "the Man upstairs." But is an altar truly an altar if nothing is offered?

After Jacob's encounter with God and his dreaded meeting with Esau, Jacob built an altar and named it Elelohe-Israel, meaning "God, the God of Israel." In effect, he was saying, "The Lord has now become the Lord of me, Israel. He is not just my father's God; he is my God!"

What was placed on that altar? In a sense it was Jacob himself. There he said his last good-bye to the old Jacob-the-deceiver, and he arose from the altar as a new man, Israel, meaning "prince of God."

On the altar of altars the Son of God was offered for us. As I look to this altar, I know, as Jacob knew, that God Almighty is also the God of me. As a believer, I have died with Christ, so I also live in Christ forever. Because Christ is risen, when we lay the old, false self on the altar, we are also raised to new life. And as we rise up off the altar, the real self that is at union with Christ is truly alive for the first time.

Jesus, "the life I live in the body, I live by faith in the Son of God, who loved me and gave himself for me" (Galatians 2:20).

Complete in Him

From the fullness of his grace we have all received one blessing after another.—John 1:16

Our completeness as individuals comes from our being joined to Christ. He fills in our empty spaces, those holes and gaps in our makeup that result from sin, and makes us whole in spirit, soul, and body.

This principle of completeness is illustrated by the mystical union of Christ and the church as a parallel to that of man and wife. "And they will become one flesh," Genesis 2:24 tells us. To separate this fusion involves ripping and tearing, because the one has literally become a part of the other. Such a painful break explains why those who go through the grief of divorce often describe it by saying, "I feel like a part of me has died."

When we come to Christ, he pours his fullness into our emptiness. That's really what it means to receive from the fullness of his grace. He who is complete joins himself to those who are incomplete so that we might be altogether and entirely whole in him.

We receive his fullness by accepting his love that surpasses knowledge, as the apostle Paul declared. As we discover and come to know the breadth, length, depth, and height of such a love, we experience "the fullness of him who fills everything in every way" (Ephesians 1:23).

Lord, thank you for the hope we have in you—the hope that there is no life so broken that you cannot mend and heal it.

No Man Is an Island

We are members of his body, of his flesh, and of his bones.
—Ephesians 5:30 KJV

"I don't need anybody. All I need is Jesus." Have you ever said or heard someone say this—or said it yourself? Usually, it's expressed by those who've experienced hurtful relationships or been burned by someone they have trusted and loved.

There are some aspects of the ministry of Christ we cannot experience in a real way except through a member of his body: someone we can touch, see, and hear—his body, his flesh, and his bones. In this way, the love of Christ is administered through our senses. We know him because we have seen him in a brother or sister.

While many believers would not receive the apostle Paul because of his former life of persecuting Christians, Barnabas administered to him God's love and acceptance. Barnabas's kindness advanced Paul's ministry in a definite way and fostered the mighty revival at Antioch.

God wants us to be interdependent, not independent. We cannot touch the literal body of Jesus, but we can experience his love through a believer's hug or touch; we can understand his grace and mercy through another's forgiveness and understanding. You will find your true identity through Jesus and his church.

Lord, you have revealed your heart to me through the members of your body. I pray that I will freely give as I have been given.

Weekend Reflections

No one is content to be a nobody, just a face or statistic. People go to great lengths to establish their worth. As someone said, "We take money we don't have to buy clothes we can't afford to impress people we don't like." Our real worth, however, should not be based on others' opinions or our own achievements but on the value God has placed on us.

Ripples of Reflection

- Jesus said, "Are not five sparrows sold for two pennies? Yet not one of them is forgotten by God. Indeed, the very hairs of your head are all numbered. Don't be afraid; you are worth more than many sparrows" (Luke 12:6–7). What promises in Scripture prove to us that God places high value on human life?

- We can't find out who we are by looking inward but only by looking up. What other false paths do we follow in trying to find ourselves?

- Think of the lies you have believed concerning what God thinks about you, then match them with the Scripture verses that refute those lies. For example: it's a lie to think, *God is too busy to care.* The truth is in Isaiah 40:28: "He will not grow tired or weary."

Hope Remains

Now these three remain: faith, hope and love. But the greatest of these is love.—1 Corinthians 13:13

Most Christians know that we cannot please God without faith and that God's very essence is love. But how many sermons are preached on hope? Yet what an important virtue it is.

Experts tell us that most depression can be best understood as anger turned inward. And what causes the anger? A situation or circumstance in which there is no hope for change. As Scripture teaches, "Hope deferred makes the heart sick, but a longing fulfilled is a tree of life" (Proverbs 13:12).

Victor Frankl, who survived the horrors of a Nazi concentration camp, said, in a speech, "I've never been here before; I've never seen any of you before; I've never given this speech before. But in my dreams, I have stood before you and said these words a thousand times." It was the hope of seeing those faces and telling that story of survival that kept him alive!

My friend, as long as you are breathing, there is still hope—hope that tomorrow will be brighter and that the sun will shine in your life again. To believe this is one of the essential virtues of the Christian life.

Lord, my hope is in you. Because I know you are alive, there is reason to be optimistic.

Endure for the Joy of It

Jesus . . . for the joy that was set before him endured the cross.—Hebrews 12:2 KJV

I'm sure you've heard the sarcastic statement after you've complained about bumping your head, "It'll feel better when it quits hurting." While this statement is said in jest, there is a principle here that rings true: sometimes we have to hurt to feel better.

Consider a surgical operation. It is something most of us would never do for fun, but we endure the pain of surgery and recovery so that we can overcome a disease or have some other problem fixed. In the same way, we sometimes must suffer through spiritual surgery to experience the thrill of victory. For a divine purpose that we cannot see, God allows crises to come into our lives. No, it is not something we enjoy, but we know the hardship is building endurance in us and bringing us to maturity.

Jesus endured the cross for the joy that awaited him. Certainly, he did not enjoy the cross, but he endured it. He gloriously triumphed over the agony of crucifixion by fixing his eyes, not on the pain and suffering, but on the joy to come. As it is written, "The joy of the LORD is your strength" (Nehemiah 8:10 KJV).

Father, when my joy is empty, your joy fills me to overflowing. Let me glimpse the glory that awaits me on the other side of the crisis I must face.

Getting to Know Him

Let us pursue the knowledge of the LORD.
—Hosea 6:3 NKJV

A young man who had recently been converted asked, "How can I grow faster? There is so much to learn and know, and I want to move forward." Certainly, not everyone who is saved is as eager to change. Nevertheless, one can grow only as quickly as the Spirit leads and guides us into all truth.

It is the daily seeking to know God that brings real change. We keep the lines open to the Spirit, saying, "God, what do you want to reveal to me today?" Then, as we listen with our hearts, we may hear his voice gently speak one word, maybe a phrase, which at the time may not seem earthshaking. But over time these little daily revelations bring a greater knowledge of our Lord. We build our knowledge of him one picture at a time, much like our earthly relationships are constructed.

God does not reveal himself to us all at once. For one thing, we simply cannot hold all of who God is. Even the great apostle Paul, after years of knowing God, said he would know him only like "a poor reflection as in a mirror" until he could see him face to face and know him "fully" (1 Corinthians 13:12).

Lord, what revelation are you bringing to my spirit?
I rejoice, knowing each discovery is a gift from you.
What joy it is to get to know you.

Ready . . . Set . . . Go!

Those who live in accordance with the Spirit have their minds set on what the Spirit desires.—Romans 8:5

*B*attle units that are thoroughly trained, frequently drilled, and always ready for action have a much better chance of survival when the enemy strikes than units that don't make preparedness a priority. Most Christians know we become new creatures when we are born again. Many do not realize, however, that it is our spirit being who then comes to life. The rest of who we are—body and soul—must die to its former nature. The mind's transformation comes when we use our wills to apply the principles in the Scriptures. The old passions and thought patterns must be cast down so that we can live by God's Word.

I've found that one of the best ways to carry out this transformation is to set my mind "on what the Spirit desires" as soon as I open my eyes each morning, before I even get out of bed. I make a conscious effort to "look to Jesus" to find the spiritual energy I'm going to need for the victories of the coming day. By following this strategy, I find that when the sinful nature cries out and conjures up its carnal passions and desires, my mind is fortified against them and better prepared to reject what is not "in accordance with the Spirit." I'm ready for battle!

Lord, keep me determined to prepare my mind for action.
Help me to be in control of myself
and to have my heart fully set on what the Spirit desires.

No Shortcuts in the Kingdom

They [train] to get a crown that will not last; but we do it to get a crown that will last forever.—1 Corinthians 9:25

Every day we are inundated with shortcuts to a goal: "Get rich quick" schemes. "Lose thirty pounds in thirty days!" "Learn a foreign language in twelve easy lessons." As the saying goes, "If it sounds too good to be true, it probably is."

There are no shortcuts to becoming a godly man or woman. It is God's way or no way. Wouldn't it be great if there were such a thing as one-step maturity? Then there would be no journey of faith, no spiritual mountains, and no adversity. Just a quick prayer and *swoop!* It would be done.

There are no such shortcuts. But that doesn't mean they won't be offered to us. You can be assured that sooner or later every man or woman of God will be tempted with an easy way to spiritual maturity. The enemy of our souls is all too happy to try and lure us into such a pursuit.

The way to godliness is training. And yet it is not the training itself that makes us godly. The training merely polishes the windows of our souls so the cleansing power of God can shine through and change us. God is the real key to godliness. If we could make ourselves godly, we wouldn't need a Savior. Only God can make us godly.

Lord, I pray that your character will show through me as I stay on the path you have chosen for me.

Weekend Reflections

In the Christian life, it's not how you start, it's how you finish. Your level of endurance is important," says Steve Farrar in his book *Point Man*. As Christians we endure difficulties because we know the end of the story. Jesus endured the cross for the joy set before him (see Hebrews 12:2). Paul pressed on for the prize (see Philippians 3:14). What hardships are you enduring? What joy do you anticipate?

Ripples of Reflection

- Jesus was offered a shortcut instead of enduring the cross. How is yielding to temptation a shortcut that leads to emptiness?

- The best things in life are most often the things that require us to work or endure. How is this evidenced in the life of the believer?

- A runner must train to endure the strain of the marathon. What can you do to strengthen your spiritual endurance?

Walking between the Lines

See to it that no one takes you captive through . . . this world rather than on Christ.—Colossians 2:8

The Christian walk at times may seem like walking between the lines, bouncing off the bumpers of grace and self-righteousness. On one side is the vain effort of man to measure up to the awesome righteousness of all that is truly holy. On the other is God's ever-abounding grace.

It is comforting to know we are not alone in this struggle. The apostle Paul wrote two very different letters to Galatia and Corinth. The church at Galatia had chosen the path of the Judaizers and were falling into the trap of the old regulations and traditions. On the other hand, the Corinthian believers had all sorts of immorality among them, and Paul rebuked them sharply.

How do we bring the two together? How do we walk in grace and follow his command, "Be ye holy; for I am holy"? (1 Peter 1:16 KJV).

It all comes back to Christ and the power of his death, burial, and resurrection working in and through us. So we look to Jesus. To nothing or no one else. We set our affections on him, as Paul said (see Colossians 3:2 KJV). Only in him do we find the power to walk between the lines.

Lord Jesus, you have called us to be holy people, and it is your presence in me that gives me the power to be holy.

The Great Exchange

He hath made him to be sin for us, . . . that we might be made the righteousness of God in him.—2 Corinthians 5:21 KJV

One of the powerful mysteries of the Bible is how, when we come to Christ in repentance, God takes our sin away and gives us his righteousness in exchange. Our bodies become God's temples, and the parts of our bodies become the members of Christ's body.

Growing up, when someone in my family was sick, my mother would put the ailing one to bed and keep the door to that room closed. She sprayed disinfectant until the whole house smelled like a hospital, and she changed the bed linens frequently, washing everything in the hottest water she could stand because she wanted to kill the germs and keep the illness from spreading to the rest of the family.

When we come to Christ, we become one with him (see 1 Corinthians 6:17). The "sickness" of our sin is laid upon him, and it becomes *his* sickness. In exchange, his righteousness becomes ours. The diseased self is consumed by the broken body of Jesus, and we receive in our spiritual veins a transfusion of the blood of Christ that gives life to the new self created in his image. As Paul said, "If anyone is in Christ, he is a new creation; the old has gone, the new has come!" (2 Corinthians 5:17).

*Lord Jesus, by faith I believe that my sin
has already been laid upon you and I have received
the gift of your righteousness in exchange.*

Starving the Old Man

When I am weak, then I am strong.—*2 Corinthians 12:10*

To be strong in the Lord is to be weak in my own strength. But how do we remain strong in the Lord on a continual rather than a temporary basis? How do we live victoriously week in and week out?

To live a Christlike life is to die to the old nature. We know this is true. But we find it harder to apply the principle than to understand it. I find it helps to think of this "dying to the old nature" as "starving the old man."

In an extended fast, the first seven days or so are the most difficult. The stomach groans and complains, like a child begging for food. Then, after the first week, the body begins to quiet down and gradually gives up its complaining. Though the desire for food is still there, it is much easier to deal with.

The same is true in the spiritual realm. As we starve the old carnal affections, they gradually become less demanding, less difficult to control. At the same time, as we nourish our spiritual side, becoming like Jesus becomes a natural instinct. As we starve our old natures, we unreservedly draw nourishment from his inexhaustible strength. And soon we find ourselves feasting at God's overflowing table of love and goodness.

Lord, feed me with your love and power
so that I can resist the old affections steadfastly,
rejoicing in my life as a new creation in you.

He Emptied Himself

Jesus was in the stern, sleeping on a cushion.—Mark 4:38

The picture of the Son of God sleeping soundly in a boat being tossed about by a tempest is thought provoking. Divinity at rest while the winds howl and men scurry about trying to adjust rigging just doesn't seem natural.

But it *was* natural. Though Jesus was God, he was also a man whose natural body got weary and needed a nap now and then. This dichotomy is something that confounds the wise. How was he God and yet man? How is it that he "emptied Himself," as the apostle Paul says, and yet remained God? (Philippians 2:7 NASB).

Suppose you were handicapped and had to walk with crutches. If I, a person with healthy legs, were to walk with crutches alongside you, it would be because I chose to do so. Though I would have the power to walk freely without the crutches, I would choose the limitation for myself. That is what Christ did. He chose to limit himself to the frailties of the human body, even though he had the power to supernaturally live in perfection.

How do we follow him in this? By choosing to serve those around us. To suffer with those who suffer. To weep with those who weep. We choose to understand so that we can better understand the heart of Jesus.

Lord, you know what it is to feel weariness, loss, and grief as well as pure joy. Keep me from selfishness at the expense of others.

Follow the Man Who Walks with a Limp

The sun rose above him as he passed Peniel, and he was limping because of his hip.—Genesis 32:31

Jacob walked differently the rest of his life after his encounter with God at Peniel, but an even bigger change occurred inside his heart. Instead of deceiving himself anymore, and rather than assuming he could weasel out of a tight situation one more time, at Peniel Jacob faced his fears alone with God. And he left as a man truly aware of his dependence on his Creator.

Show me someone who is successful and has never experienced any defeat or failure, then show me someone who has triumphed over disappointment, fear, or failure, and ask me which person I would follow into the storm. Always, my answer is the same: I'd follow the one who walks with a limp. Who wants to follow someone who has never faced his or her greatest enemy, the false self? Who will follow a person who has never trembled in the darkness, never cried, never been afraid? Is that person really a leader to be followed?

Some of the most mature men and women of God have waged the tough battle and emerged stronger and more holy, yet encumbered by a limp. These are the believers who know Christ more intimately because they have shared with him in his suffering (see Romans 8:17).

Jesus, you are the ultimate example of a man unashamed of his scars. Let me bear the marks of one who has walked with you.

269

Weekend Reflections

Of all the names God uses to describe himself, one of my favorites is Holy. According to one Hebrew source, it generally means "set apart, consecrated." To many, the holiness of God is a subject full of dread and fear. But as children of God we should have a holy fear for God, not a dreadful fear. His wrath has been appeased through the work of the Cross (see 1 Thessalonians 5:9).

Ripples of Reflection

- Is the holiness of God something you fear? If so, why?

- What would be the dangers of serving a God who was not holy?

- How can we be holy as he has commanded us to be?

Belonging to Christ

*You do not belong to the world, but I have chosen you
out of the world.—John 15:19*

In relationships there are different levels of commitment. For example, at work the employer-to-employee relationship is based on the employee's level of performance. The boss promises, "As long as you carry out your responsibilities, I will see that you are compensated." In friendships, relationships may be based on a commitment to sharing common interests. Unfortunately, for too many couples the marriage relationship is a commitment to stay in the marriage until one of the spouses gets bored with the arrangement.

Our relationship to Christ is different from these earthly commitments. When we say we belong to him, we're talking about a long-term, lifetime commitment. God has made a covenant with us. He is committed to seeing us through the process of becoming more like him until Christ's nature is completely formed in us. Even when we are ready to give up on ourselves, God never gives up on us. His words should forever ring in our hearts: "Can a mother forget the baby at her breast and have no compassion on the child she has borne? Though she may forget, I will not forget you!" (Isaiah 49:15).

*Lord, I praise you for your unfailing love.
There is never a time that you have forgotten about me.
Thank you for being that kind of God!*

He'll Never Let You Go

He will [march] with you; He will not fail you or let you go or forsake you.—Deuteronomy 31:8 AMP

These were the words of Moses to his beloved friend and aide, Joshua. Moses knew his death was approaching. Now Joshua would have to lead the people into the Promised Land. He would have to finish what Moses could not do.

Joshua needed Moses's firm words of encouragement. He needed to be told again that God would be with him just as he had been with Moses. He needed that same assurance that God would remain faithful.

When we face changes in life, we often start grasping for what we feel is secure, something that will not change. We may look to a trusted loved one, such as a spouse, mother, or father, or to an older mentor or a long-time friend. In times of radical change, such as the death of a spouse or a child, we desperately cling to the one who will not change. Like Joshua, we need to hear again the words of Moses, to be told again that God "will not fail you or let you go."

There is no arm as strong as our God's, no hand that grips so surely. He has a firm hold on you, and he will never let you go—no matter where you go, no matter what you may face, no matter what changes come.

Father, I will run to you in time of trouble and hide in the shadow of your wings (see Psalm 57:1).

One-on-One

But Noah found grace in the eyes of the LORD.
—Genesis 6:8 KJV

Before God destroyed the earth with the great flood, he saw a corrupt world, the wickedness of man. Everywhere God looked he saw rebellion and depravity—everywhere, that is, except in one man: Noah. God saved Noah and his family because of Noah's faithfulness.

When we consider God's greatness, his immeasurable power and ability, the idea that he can see us as individuals seems out of reach. It is easier to think of God as one who relates to us corporately rather than one-on-one. The fact is, though, that God knows us individually, just as he knew Noah. And he loves each of us in our own right. Each one of us is special to him.

Consider this as your challenge: realize the vastness of God's mental capacity; it's greater than anything you can ever imagine, big enough to manage a universe. And yet God's mind can linger with you at any time. We may have difficulty doing two things at once, but God is without limits. He can do all things at once—and still know us as intimately as a Creator knows his creation.

To God, no one job requires any more effort than another. Nothing is a task. He is in perfect control of this cosmos, and he still has time to listen and keep his eyes on you.

Lord, there is not a time that I am out of your sight.
I am not a statistic or number in your kingdom
but a child that you know by name.

Does God Sleep In on Mondays?

Behold, he that keepeth Israel shall neither slumber nor sleep.—Psalm 121:4 KJV

Oh, those Sundays! The worship days when the very heavens seem to open and God seems close enough to touch, when we shake the rafters with our Lord's Day songs of praise. Then comes Monday, and suddenly we feel so terribly unspiritual.

From time to time all of us struggle to sense the supernatural in the ordinary daily grind, especially, it seems, on Mondays. We long to see the miraculous in the mediocre, to bring a little Sunday heaven into the weekday blahs, but sometimes it's awfully hard to do. Do you ever wonder if God hides from us on Mondays?

No, he is there on our moody Mondays as well as our super Tuesdays, wonderful Wednesdays, troublesome Thursdays, and frustrated Fridays. He doesn't live at church. He isn't with us only when we are feeling spiritual; he's our Friend, our Spirit, our Comforter twenty-four hours a day, seven days a week. His mercies are new every morning.

He is there with us through it all. In our joy he smiles with us. In our sadness he weeps with us. He is a God who is intimately involved in the routine humdrum of our daily lives as well as the intricate workings of the cosmos. Even on Monday mornings. Because God never sleeps in.

Oh Lord Jesus, open my heart to sense you in the everyday, to walk by faith when there is no feeling.

God Is Not Surprised!

Don't be surprised at the fiery trials you are going through.
—1 Peter 4:12 NLT

*S*ometimes life catches us unaware and jolts us into believing that our lives are spinning out of control. I recall one dear saint who asked for prayer one day after a midweek Bible study. With tearful emotion she said, "My children are grown and have their own lives now. When they were at home, I knew my purpose was to be the best mother I could. But now they're gone, and I don't know why I'm here."

I wondered what I could say to help relieve her distress. Then I heard that small voice inside me saying, "Tell her I am not surprised."

The depth of meaning in those few words brought great comfort to her—and to myself as well. Although we might be surprised by the circumstances that swirl through our lives, God is not. He lovingly holds our hands and leads us. "Walk on, child," he tells us. "I know the plan I have for you, and you're going to be just fine!"

No matter how chaotic it may feel, your life is not out of control. If you are walking in covenant with God, he will be faithful. He knows where you are; he has ordered the steps of your life (see Psalm 37:23 KJV). He knows the path you will take, and he is not anxious or weary.

Oh Father, what comfort it is to know that I cannot escape from your presence. I know you have plans to prosper me.

Weekend Reflections

Questions will come. Voices will call us to doubt God's faithfulness. But when worry torments us, we should stop and realize that the one whose purpose we are questioning is the one who hung the stars on nothing, carved the landscape with his word, and breathed our spirits into existence. How can we expect to completely understand his methods when we behold his genius, his omnipotence in all he has performed?

Ripples of Reflection

- Look at nature and identify how creation points to God's faithfulness (for example, the rainbow, the seasons, the stars).

- The apostle Paul said, "The one who calls you is faithful and he will do it" (1 Thessalonians 5:24). What has God called you to do? How are you leaning on his faithfulness to "do it"?

- Faithfulness depends on character. God will keep his part of the covenant. What is your part? (see 2 Chronicles 6:14).

The Terrible World of the Ungrateful

People will be . . . proud, abusive, disobedient to their parents, ungrateful, unholy.—2 Timothy 3:2

*I*t's interesting that Paul, describing a scene of gross immorality and depraved minds, included among the sins of men who were "without excuse" (Romans 1:20) the fact that they "neither were thankful" (verse 21 KJV).

We all know people who are never thankful. Who enjoys the company of such people? Their ungratefulness spills over into their general attitude toward life.

Corrie ten Boom learned the power of thankfulness in the comfortless conditions of a flea-infested prison camp. In her book *The Hiding Place*, she said that one day she and her sister, Betsie, were reading 1 Thessalonians 5:18—"In every thing give thanks" (KJV)—when Betsie encouraged her to give thanks for the fleas. It was only after her sister's persistence over several months that Corrie finally relented and thanked God for the pests. Sometime later they learned they had been able to study the Bible and pray without interference because the guards would not enter the barracks due to the fleas.

Are you having a problem with gloominess and despair? Try expressing more gratitude, first to God and then to others. Pray your thanks aloud. Your ears need to hear it too!

Father, I choose to be thankful today. You are a gracious God whose love endures forever. Great is your faithfulness to me.

Holding On with a Loose Grip

Instead, you ought to say, "If it is the Lord's will, we will live and do this or that."—James 4:15

The longer I live, the more I have come to believe that nothing is permanent—except maybe "permanent press." Everything else is subject to change. The sooner we realize this, the less life will take us by surprise.

When it comes to life and people, anything can happen. It is a mistake to base your life on present circumstances. Go ahead and make plans, but realize there may have to be adjustments. The sooner you can accept this fact, the sooner you will have peace.

God is a God of vision and purpose. He wants us to set goals and make plans—as long as we recognize his sovereignty as the highest authority. Remember: "Many are the plans in a man's heart, but it is the Lord's purpose that prevails" (Proverbs 19:21).

Whether it is wealth, children, or a job, all our blessings are gifts from God. We must enjoy them today, because only God knows about tomorrow. If you are going to grip anything tightly, let it be the hand of God. Hold everything else with an open hand. Then if your other hand becomes empty, your balance will remain steady because you are holding something that never changes.

The earth is yours, Lord, including everything you have given me. Family, friends, and things are gifts you have allowed me to hold for a while.

What Kind of House Are You Building?

The fire will test the quality of each man's work.
—1 Corinthians 3:13

*I*n the small town where I was raised, I stood beside a classmate as we watched her home burn. The girl wept, not for the house so much as for things that couldn't be replaced. "Pictures," I heard her say.

Throughout our lifetimes you and I are building "houses," but they are houses we cannot really see with natural eyes. From time to time we get a glimpse of the evidence of the houses, but there is only one who truly sees them. One day, though, we will know for certain what we have used to build our houses, whether we have built them with the things that will endure or with temporary pleasures. We will know whether we have used gold and silver or wood and straw "because the Day will bring it to light" (1 Corinthians 3:13). God will test it with his fire on the day of judgment. Those things done for the praise of men or for selfish gain will be burned up. That's the wood and straw. But whatever is done for the glory of God will stand and remain.

Next time you do something you think is of value, ask yourself, *Is this wood and hay, or is it gold and silver?* Have you stopped to look at your spiritual house?

Oh God, I want to build things that will stand the test of your fire. Don't let me waste time on houses of hay and stubble.

Embrace It!

Be thankful.—Colossians 3:15

While some things are sure in the Christian life—salvation, God's faithfulness, daily provision, heaven—there are other things we may dream of that will never happen. If we knew all things, we probably would thank God that he did not give us everything we dreamed of!

Don't postpone your life until some perfect time or place in the future. That time or place may never come. Don't put off getting involved in a church until you find the perfect congregation "where people are more loving and committed." Don't put off living, thinking, *If I just had a different spouse . . .* or, *If only I could be shorter, taller, thinner . . .* I am not making light of these desires. I know these issues have brought much heartache to some people. But, my friend, the truth is that God is God of the present. For whatever reason, he has allowed you to be at this place and time with these circumstances, and his peace will come to you when you embrace life in the here and now.

Your situation may change. Your dreams may all come true. But if the sun doesn't come out, if your dreams don't come true, live today anyway. Do all you can to enjoy this moment God has given you. Be thankful for it! Embrace it!

Lord, I must admit I don't always understand,
but I thank you for what you have given me here and now.
I will live and find the beauty in today.

Have You Heard the Secret?

I have learned the secret of being content in any and every situation, whether . . . in plenty or in want.—Philippians 4:12

It's easy to feel that whatever we have is never enough. We get a raise, then we buy more stuff. Then we need another raise to pay for the maintenance of the new stuff. So we buy some maintenance stuff to take care of the old stuff. Then we need another raise to maintain the new maintenance stuff . . . and the cycle goes on.

In contrast to this endless cycle of want, the trademark of the godly person is contentment. Whether this person has little or much, he or she is at peace.

This is not something that just happens, like receiving salvation or being healed. It is something a godly person learns. Even the great apostle Paul said, "I have learned the secret." Paul knew what it was like to have plenty of stuff, and he knew what it was like to need stuff. And in both places he found a secret.

What secret of contentment was he referring to? It was the fact that he was strengthened by Christ himself: "I can do everything through him who gives me strength" (Philippians 4:13). Now it is no longer a secret. Paul has shared his knowledge with us.

Though I may not know how to do it yet, I am learning to be content—whether I have a lot of stuff or I think I need a few more things.

Father, only you really know what I need, and you know before I ask. You graciously supply my needs according to your great riches.

Weekend Reflections

Gerald Mann wrote, "In every tragedy you can look at what you've lost and be hateful, or you can look at what you have left and be grateful. Joseph (Old Testament) was a grand example of choosing to be grateful instead of hateful in the face of betrayal" (*When the Bad Times Are Over for Good*).

There is a cure for those afflicted with the disease of self-pity. It's called thankfulness. It is by expressing thanks for what we do have that our eyes are lifted from ourselves to what is lovely, good, and right. Suddenly what we don't have or what we cannot have loses its power over us, and we find the courage to be a giver and not just a receiver.

Ripples of Reflection

- Spend an hour thinking about everything you are thankful for. Gauge the difference in your attitude at the beginning and at the end of that time.

- Think of those who seem to be the most joyful and content. How big a part does thankfulness play in their lives? What about those who are miserable?

- How does being unthankful lead to a more sinful state? (see Romans 1:21–32).

Just Say No

The grace of God . . . teaches us to say "No" to ungodliness and worldly passions.—Titus 2:11–12

One of the first words we try to teach children to understand is the word *no*. From the moment they eagerly look at those basement steps, we earnestly hope they will quickly learn to obey.

A good friend of mine attempted to teach his two-year-old the significance of this word as the child repeatedly tried to stick things into the electrical outlets. Unfortunately, the word *no* didn't suffice, and when Dad wasn't looking, the child got a shocking surprise! The youngster learned the advantages of obedience the hard way. Much like that little child, we sometimes fail to heed the voice of God in our hearts saying no as he tries to teach us lessons for living.

We are God's children, learning to be more like him, but we're still in training. We aren't there yet. Like my friend's little child, we hear his voice in our heart, but sometimes we just don't listen. Or perhaps we can't quite accept that God is right; we can't see how this one little thing could be wrong. If we heed God's voice instructing us, we don't have to learn the hard way, nor do we have to be burned by the enemy's fire. God, in his grace, is teaching us to obey . . . by saying no.

Father, teach me that sometimes all I need to do is just say no. Keep me from the evil one. Let me walk circumspectly, aware of his devices.

Forward Ho!

. . . being confident of this, that he who began a good work in
you will carry it on to completion.—Philippians 1:6

I have always been fascinated by the clipper ship. There is something so free and inviting about the vessel's grand sails, stretched taut, welcoming the winds of the sea. The ship doesn't sail under its own power, so there's no engine noise. Just the sound of the sails snapping out in the breeze and the splashes of the hull cutting through the waves of the briny deep.

We should remember that, like the clipper ship, we do not move under our own power but by the power of the Holy Spirit. We just exert our wills—lift our sails—to be controlled by the Spirit's leading.

Have you longed to reach a point in your life when you feel complete as a Christian, fulfilled and enriched with God's plan for your life? Have you ever felt frustrated, thinking, *I'll never get there?* Take heart. Lift your sails, open your heart, and let the Spirit move you toward completion. God's purpose in your life will be fulfilled, and your destiny will be realized. God is seeing to it that the work that was begun carries on day by day until the prize is obtained, the destination is reached.

If your goal is to become like Jesus, God is working in you to see that you attain that goal.

Father, I believe I will see the day when your work
is completed and a new one is begun and that
together we will walk from glory to glory.

From Ordinary to Extraordinary

Those God foreknew he also predestined to be conformed to the likeness of his Son.—Romans 8:29

Before a sculptor ever begins to sculpt, he or she pictures what the end will be. Everything the artist does to the stone or wood conforms to that mental image of the end product. God works the same way in our lives. God sees us with the end in mind.

This is why Jesus called as his disciples such ordinary men—not the scholars and wise men of the day but seemingly common men who had an extraordinary propensity to "become." Jesus saw what they could be. He looked at Peter and said, "Upon this rock I will build my church; and the gates of hell shall not prevail against it" (Matthew 16:18 KJV). Peter—the same man Jesus rebuked a few verses later for his hasty speech. Jesus saw Peter's weaknesses, but he also saw the man who would one day be willing to give his life for the gospel.

If we could only see the end of our lives as well as the present! If we could only realize the power that is working in us and understand what it's capable of doing in our lives! It is the same power that raised Jesus from the dead! Just imagine: that power is alive and working in us right now, conforming us to the heavenly design and purpose that God has fashioned.

Father, your purpose for me is what I want.
You have the ending of my story in mind,
but I know it's up to me to embrace your plan for me.

Come On In!

Him that cometh to me I will in no wise cast out.
—John 6:37 KJV

*D*id you ever have one of those teachers in school who simply refused to help? Who denied that you could be having trouble understanding? "Don't worry about it," he or she would say. "Just hang in there; you'll get it." How fortunate we are that our heavenly teacher is not that way. When we boldly come before the throne of grace, he smiles and says, "Come on in!" In contrast to those teachers and friends who are intolerant of our slow progress, Jesus is patient, "full of compassion, and gracious, longsuffering, and plenteous in mercy and truth" (Psalm 86:15 KJV).

It is interesting to note that the Greek word translated as "no wise" in John 6:37 is *ou nay*, a double negative. Jesus was saying emphatically, "I will never, no never, reject one of them who comes to Me" (AMP).

We say, "Lord, I'm back again. I . . . I didn't get it." But if we come to the Lord twenty times in a single day, it's not a nuisance to him. He realizes our helpless state. That is why he came to earth, to empower us to do what we could not do ourselves. God is glorified in our weakness. It is in our needful state that his strength is revealed.

Lord Jesus, I choose to come to your throne of grace. Where else can I go? Your kindness draws me to you (see Romans 2:4).

Grow Up? But How?

Like newborn babies, crave pure spiritual milk, so that by it you may grow up in your salvation.—1 Peter 2:2

Children are children because that is all they know how to be. No matter how frustrated parents become with their children, the children cannot become adults until the appointed time. They will continue to make mistakes and think only of themselves until they mature to the next season of life.

The same is true in the spiritual realm. At the point of exasperation we may want to shout at new believers, "Grow up!" But new believers who are beginning the Christian journey will not walk as mature believers. There are some things they have not learned yet.

Parents learn to focus on their children's behavior or the attitude that needs adjusting so that step by step and lesson by lesson the children grow into adulthood. Normal parents love their children in spite of their failures and inabilities; parents accept the fact that their children are works in progress.

So, Mom and Dad, let your children be children. This stage passes too quickly anyway; enjoy the process. And, brother or sister in Christ, let us be patient with our baby brothers and sisters. They will grow up—at the appointed time.

Father, I'm your child. I know how patient you have been with me, so I will be patient with others.

Weekend Reflections

*T*he gospel of the kingdom advances itself. Wherever it takes root, purity and righteousness will grow and spread. Your personal spiritual growth is nurtured by the power of God's good news being planted in you. As the apostle Paul said, "All over the world this gospel is bearing fruit and growing, just as it has been doing among you since the day you heard it and understood God's grace in all its truth" (Colossians 1:6).

Ripples of Reflection

- If your growth depends on where you are planted, what is your responsibility?

- To grow, we must be willing to change. What positive changes have occurred in your life in the last six months?

- The strong oak tree is a slow grower. Are you willing to be patient with others and with yourself as you grow in strength and maturity? What will be the evidence of this?

God's Growing Church

You are Peter, and on this rock I will build my church.
—Matthew 16:18

*R*est assured, Jesus is building his church at this very moment. Despite the inadequacy of mankind, our failures and weaknesses, God's plan is on schedule, because it is God's church, and he is building it "on this rock."

And what is "this rock"? I believe it is the revelation knowledge of Jesus Christ—not just the knowledge that he is the Son of God but a continual revealing of Christ's nature, character, and power. This is not knowledge in the scientific sense but in the discerning sense. I don't claim to be a Greek scholar, even at the most elementary level, but I believe the Greek word used here does not describe mental knowledge but a knowledge that takes place at the heart level. If our knowledge—our revelation of Jesus—is not growing, then we can assume we are not growing, period. If a church's revelation of Jesus is not growing, then most likely the church is not growing in numbers or otherwise. As the wise man said, "By wisdom a house is built, and through understanding it is established; through knowledge its rooms are filled with rare and beautiful treasures" (Proverbs 24:3–4).

Oh Lord Jesus, that I might have a fresh revelation of your
brilliance, your majesty, your power.
I wait now for a word from you.

The Great Pretenders

His enemy came and sowed tares among the wheat.
—Matthew 13:25 NKJV

At one time or another we've all said, "How could I have been so blind?" We've all been fooled. Sadly, we're sometimes deceived by people even within the church; there are great pretenders there too. In his parable regarding the kingdom of heaven, Jesus made it clear that the wheat are his children and the tares are the pretenders the enemy has strategically placed among his people.

I have met those dear, disillusioned saints who wearily wander from church to church, looking for one with no pretenders. If you're one of those wanderers, hang it up. There ain't one! (Excuse the slang.) As long as Satan is on the prowl and human beings exist on earth, there will be pretenders. But we can take comfort in knowing that God can tell the difference. He knows who's pretending and who isn't. His church is secure. As the apostle Paul wrote to young Timothy, "God's solid foundation stands firm, sealed with this inscription: 'The Lord knows those who are his'" (2 Timothy 2:19).

Lord, I trust you to separate the tares from the wheat, so in the end "the righteous will shine like the sun" (Matthew 13:43).

One Big Family

You have come to Mount Zion, to the heavenly Jerusalem, the city of the living God.—Hebrews 12:22

Are you looking for a city where there are no fatherless children and no childless moms and dads? There is one. But you can't just go visit it. This is a members-only kind of place. But once you become a member, you can live there forever. And when you're there, you are never alone. You belong to a family that is innumerable.

The writer of Hebrews reminded the believers that they were not heading toward a place that could be touched or a place of darkness, gloom, and storm. He was referring to Israel's fearful encounter with God at Mount Sinai, but in this case he was not speaking of a literal mountain or city but of a spiritual kingdom filled with "thousands upon thousands of angels in joyful assembly, . . . the church of the firstborn, whose names are written in heaven" (Hebrews 12:22–23).

This is the heritage we have as believers. We don't have to divide it up into shares; we get it all! In God's sight every believer has the same rights. It's as though we all get all the privileges of the firstborn. There are no seconds or thirds, no oldest and youngest, no unwanted offspring—only children who are loved and blessed, each one as if he or she were an only child.

God, you have called us your sons and daughters. Thank you for the wonderful family you have birthed me into.

Is Church Boring to You?

He that believeth on me, as the scripture hath said, out of his belly shall flow rivers of living water.—John 7:38 KJV

From time to time I hear brothers and sisters in Christ say something like this: "I just don't get anything out of church anymore. I'm just kind of bored with it." I can appreciate the frankness of someone who "tells it like it is." However, upon closer examination of those sentiments, I have to wonder whether this person's boredom is actually the work of the Spirit in his or her life. (I heard that gasp!) Maybe God has allowed church to get boring for a reason.

You see, God never meant for church services to be the end of it all. The church is where we get equipped to go out and do the works of Jesus. Only as the life of God flows out of you will it flow into you. The Holy Spirit was not given just for our benefit and enjoyment. He did not come just so we would get together in church and feel goose bumps when the singing is especially beautiful and the preaching is especially effective. The Holy Spirit came to empower us to do the works of Jesus in the earth! We're the conduits through which the living water is to flow into the world. So if you don't feel anything coming in, examine what's going out!

Lord, count me in. I want to be one the river flows through.

Unanswered Prayer

. . . that they all may be one; as thou, Father, art in me, and I in thee, that they also may be one in us.—John 17:21 KJV

*M*any times we hear nonbelievers say, "How can there be a God when there are so many different churches? They can't all be right!"

Considering the multitude of denominations, it's easy to see how non-Christians are confused in their search for truth. The world will be more receptive to the gospel when churches are more receptive to one another.

When he was here on earth, Jesus prayed we would all become one church, "that the world may believe that thou hast sent me" (John 17:21 KJV). Because Christ could see through time, he saw the splintered, twentieth-century church, and he prayed that it could be mended so the hurting and needy could find a safe place to be restored to life again. This prayer still goes unanswered.

Christians do not need to agree on every point to be the one body of Christ. We just need to sincerely share Christ's love with one another and unite in areas where we can make a difference. We must come together and stand on the foundation that has been laid, the Cornerstone, Christ Jesus our Lord. There we will find a solid Rock that is stable and secure. As we stand together, *we* will be the answer to our Lord's prayer.

Jesus, make us one, even as you and the Father are one.
Bring your church together so that the world may believe
and receive the gospel.

Weekend Reflections

All that is truly good in life is a gift from God. The beauty of creation and of people demonstrate the creativity and artistry of an amazing God. No one person completely reveals the character and beauty of God's personality except Christ. As Scripture tells us, "The Son is the radiance of God's glory and the exact representation of his being, sustaining all things by his powerful word" (Hebrews 1:3). True Christians are all members of the same body; it takes all of us together to illustrate his body (see 1 Corinthians 12:7). No one church or people can fully reveal Christ to the world.

Ripples of Reflection

- Reflect on this week's readings, noting the believers who have demonstrated a certain aspect of God's character to you.

- Observe the various traits in the different cultures that may be around you, and consider how they may be useful in revealing Christ to the world.

- If every Christian were exactly like you, what demonstration of God's nature to the world would be missing? (for example, boldness, serenity, cheerfulness, affection, etc.)

Beyond Knowledge

I pray that you . . . may . . . know this love that surpasses knowledge.—Ephesians 3:17–19

As Christians we know and believe that God loves us. We acknowledge his faithful, undying love for the Jewish nation as he delivered them from Egypt, and we comprehend the fact that his love for all the world was displayed on a hill called Golgotha.

But God's love goes way beyond knowledge. It cannot be confined in the work of a thousand commentaries and Bible-study helps. It spills over the boundaries, disregarding man's intelligence and wisdom, splashing delightfully through the corridors of the hearts of those who pursue it. This love cannot be understood, but it can be experienced in the depth of our souls as our spirits celebrate deep communion with the Holy One.

Sometimes, in prayer, with tears streaming down our faces and emotions so intense that words just don't come, we sense his love reaching out to us in ways that cannot be comprehended through mere intellect—for the intensity of his love is beyond knowing. And without any spoken communication, we commune with our Creator on a higher plane. We feel our spirits yearning within us, crying, "Abba, Abba!" And we know we have connected with the love of God in a way that surpasses knowledge.

Oh, the boundless love of God! Thank you, God, that there are always greater realms of your love to be revealed.

Forbearance

Be completely humble and gentle; be patient, bearing with one another in love.—Ephesians 4:2

Many believers make the mistake of believing that God works with all of us in the same way, disregarding the fact that he considers each person's level of maturity in his dealings with us. God is looking for the best that each of us *can* do, not what we think that person *should* be doing. He is the all-knowing Father who understands that each of his children is unique. In contrast, Satan wants us to waste all our time fighting with one another about our differences so we forget who our real enemy is.

God's church should be a family—a place where all his different children, the godly and obedient as well as the wounded and oppressed—can come and find peace. But instead of being a haven of rest, sometimes the church is more like a den of strife, where peace is just a pause between arguments.

God's true love is forbearing, "ready to believe the best of every person" (1 Corinthians 13:7 AMP). As Paul wrote to the Ephesians, God is our peace, the one who tore down the "dividing wall of hostility" (Ephesians 2:14). Let's leave that wall down and follow our Father's example.

Jesus, you are the one who destroyed the walls of division between your people. Give us grace to forbear with each other as we grow up into you.

He's Got the Whole World in His Hand

The earth is the LORD's, and everything in it. The world and all its people belong to him.—Psalm 24:1 NLT

Travel virtually anywhere, and you will find tragedy. In certain countries of Africa, the AIDS epidemic is so great that the government can't build enough hospitals for the victims to die in. There are countries where ten-year-olds become prostitutes to support their families. In other nations parents willingly give their children to temple priests so the family can receive absolution for crimes committed.

Such atrocities shock us and break our hearts. We weep. We send money. We go to the ends of the earth to try and help, and yet the tragedies continue. Still, our Father has called us to heal the sick, to bear one another's burden, to give to the poor—and we must obey.

When we feel that our efforts are insignificant, we must remember that God doesn't expect us to heal the world all by ourselves, but he reminds us that even a "cup of water" in Christ's name will not go unseen by heaven's eyes (see Mark 9:41).

God is orchestrating a symphony of love. While one Christian ministers to a dying AIDS patient, another translates the Scriptures for a tribe of primitive people. While one holds a baby born addicted to drugs, another gives a cup of cool water to a thirsty child. We do what we can while recognizing there is only one Lord of the harvest, and it's not one of us. God is the one who gives the increase.

Father, you know each helpless child and hurting heart by name. Not one of them hurts without your knowledge.

Jesus Is Loving You!

You are the body of Christ, and each one of you is a part of it.—1 Corinthians 12:27

Those who know Wayne Francis have endearingly nicknamed him Saint Francis. It's nearly impossible for anyone to be around Wayne very long before he finds a way to minister to that person. Whether in a practical or a spiritual way, he inevitably reveals his heart for others—buying a meal, offering up a prayer, leading someone to Christ, or simply speaking God's Word in a fresh way.

Most of us admire folks like Wayne and want to be around them. They have learned to manifest the nature of Christ and have become conduits of God's living water to the world. When we're with them, they energize and inspire us, and we feel like better people.

We all want to be assured that God knows our names and where we live. While we are looking for some miraculous sign—an angel, a flash of light, or a voice in the night—God's love and concern for us are quite evident in the common people he sends to minister to us. They live out his life-giving words in kindness to others.

The warmth and love we sense from the pure in heart is Christ's warmth and love. The goodness that flows from these brothers and sisters is none other than the goodness of Christ himself. It flows from his fountain through them as a blessing to us. It is Jesus himself, loving us through a member of his body.

Dear God, thank you for those you have sent to speak your word into my life. I know, Lord, that it is really you shining through them.

A Passionate God

When God created man, he made him in the likeness of God.
—Genesis 5:1

God loves. He hates. He laughs. He cries. He embraces. He kisses. He shouts. He whispers. He sings. He grieves (see John 3:16, Proverbs 6:16, Psalm 2:4, John 11:35, Luke 15:20, Jeremiah 25:30, 1 Kings 19:12, Zephaniah 3:17, and 1 Chronicles 21:15).

Some reject such a passionate God, preferring, instead, a God who is detached and tucked away in a cathedral where they can go visit him. Don't give them a God who is active, intimate, and passionate. After all, how could God be truly God and have those kinds of passions?

Where do you think we got the capacity to love, hate, weep, and rejoice, if not from our Father? We were created in his likeness (see Genesis 5:1). It was God himself who placed our complex souls in us. And if we have the capacity for such passions, God's passions must be infinitely beyond our own.

Just imagine the heaviest grief you have known. Jesus sorrowed more. Remember your highest joys? His joy is fuller still. Think of the times you were angered because of the lack of justice for the innocent. God was angered more. Imagine the greatest love you have seen demonstrated, then know that God's love is deeper, higher, longer, and wider than that—and purer.

Lord Jesus, give me a greater understanding of who you are. Help me grasp the fact that you don't just extend love to us; you are love.

Weekend Reflections

God's love is the forbearing kind, "ready to believe the best of every person" (1 Corinthians 13:7 AMP). Instead of seeing us in our weakness, God's love sees our needs.

Ripples of Reflection

- We are commanded to love as we have been loved (see John 13:34). Considering the qualities of Christ's love for us, how should we love others?

- Jesus loves us through others. Thinking back over this week, how has Christ loved you through someone else.

- The Bible tells us God's love cannot be confined to knowledge (see Ephesians 3:19). How, then, do we comprehend this love?

Choose Joy!

Be joyful at your Feast.—Deuteronomy 16:14

*B*eing joyful is more of a decision than a feeling. Sometimes the decision to be joyful takes effort. Christmas may be one of those times.

Christmas is a time for celebration, good cheer, and joy. But just because it's the time for those feelings doesn't mean we automatically feel them. Tragedy or disappointment may have knocked the wind out of you, leaving you feeling anything but joyful. But there is still reason to rejoice. If you are struggling with pain or sorrow as the holiday approaches, I urge you to awaken your heart and hear the "good tidings of great joy" (Luke 2:10 KJV).

The news the angels brought to the shepherds was not just to herald Christ's birth for the world, but to say, "Today . . . a Savior has been born to you" (verse 11). Your reason to rejoice on Christmas Day is that Christ was born for you as much as for anyone else in the world. And one of the reasons Emmanuel came to be with us is to bring us comfort and joy. Lay aside the hurt that overshadows your joy. Celebrate the birth of the one who came to take your burdens upon himself. Make a conscious decision to let his peace and joy fill your heart.

Lord Jesus, the joy I have is more than a feeling of Christmas spirit. It is birthed from the realization that you were born for even me.

A Heart Full of Treasures

Mary treasured up all these things and pondered them in her heart.—Luke 2:19

Some things seem to lose some of their loveliness when they are flaunted publicly. They are meant to be treasured in our heart.

Have you ever been around a married couple when they start discussing their personal business in front of you? Feels awkward, doesn't it? The Spirit sometimes reveals to me things that are too personal to become common knowledge. They are part of my private conversations with God, topics reserved for personal discussions with my Creator.

Perhaps God shares some things with you, too, that are not meant to be shared with the whole world or even with your circle of friends and family members. God may want you to show some restraint and keep those things between you and him. That was true for the apostle Paul. In 2 Corinthians 12:4 he said he heard things in heavenly places that "man is not permitted to tell."

When they are treasured and spoken at the right time, words have a beauty they would not have if they were pretentiously trumpeted about. They become like the king's crown jewels, displayed only for the right occasion, or "like apples of gold in settings of silver" (Proverbs 25:11 NKJV).

Lord Jesus, grant me the discernment to know what things I should ponder in my heart and what things should be shared with others.

When God Rejoiced

He will take great delight in you, . . . he will rejoice over you with singing.—Zephaniah 3:17

Children know how to rejoice. Just visit a classroom on the day before Christmas vacation. Adults, on the other hand, rarely rejoice. Think about it. When was the last time you rejoiced? What was the occasion?

I grew up in a culture that generally considered rejoicing rather uncouth. Especially if it were done openly—and even more so if the rejoicer was a man. A man who exuberantly rejoiced in public was considered immature and silly.

In contrast, it's interesting to see what God has chosen to rejoice about. In Luke 10:21, Jesus rejoiced because the Father chose to reveal the working of the kingdom to "little children" and let it be hidden from the wise. This is the same God who splashed the sky with stars, rolled out the universe, and stooped to breathe into Adam's nostrils the breath of life—and then simply said that it was "good." Instead, he gets excited about simple people becoming partakers of his heritage, about one sinner repenting, about one prodigal son finding his way home, about one sheep returning to the flock.

Think about these things that God rejoiced over. Then think about the last time you rejoiced enough to cause someone to notice.

Father, every day there is reason to rejoice. Let me celebrate the things you celebrate and delight in what you love.

What's in a Name?

God . . . gave him the name that is above every name.
—Philippians 2:9

*P*arents spend hours choosing names for their babies because a name is closely linked to their child's character. The Bible teaches us that God began his covenant with man by naming himself. God's name was revealed first; it was not given to him by some man. Those names came later, when great men walked with God and began to know him. For example, when God provided a ram for Abraham, Abraham called God *Jehovah-Jireh*, meaning "God, my provider." And as God was revealed, he was also named *Jehovah-Roi*, meaning "God, my shepherd," and *Jehovah-Shalom*, meaning "God, my peace."

The prophets saw glimpses of the future when God said he would reveal himself by a mightier name that they could not know. Today we have the privilege of knowing that name: Jesus.

Do you know why there is such power in Jesus's name? Because God gave it to him: "Therefore God exalted him to the highest place and gave him the name that is above every name, that at the name of Jesus every knee should bow" (Philippians 2:9–10).

God has been revealed as our Jesus, which means he is our Savior. But unless you have received the revelation of him into your own life, Jesus is just a name.

God, I willingly bow my knee today and worship his name,
for you have always been God, but now you are my Savior.
You are my Jesus.

God with Me

They shall call his name Emmanuel, which being interpreted is,
God with us.—Matthew 1:23 KJV

For generations men and women longed for God. Isaiah was one of the select few who saw him. Along with other men of renown, like Moses, Abraham, and Jacob, Isaiah saw God and conversed with him in a real way.

I wonder what it was like to see this God they had prayed and sacrificed to, the God they had heard about and feared, the one behind the awesome displays of power they had witnessed. Finally, he stood before them and talked with them.

Only a few such events were recorded for thousands of years. Then God surprised all of humanity and appeared, not to only a few, but to the world—as a baby! He would grow up to be a man who would walk, talk, and eat as all people do. His body of flesh would be subject to the same frailties as ours. He would get drowsy, even exhausted, feel the sting of pain, and the aching of grief. He would be God . . . with us and like us.

And now, the wonder of that awesome truth becomes even more astonishing: he is not only God with us but God with *me*. He is not just a God who visits me when I pray or sees me when I go to church. He is with me always! I am never really alone, because God—my God and yours too—is with me.

Lord Jesus, I thank you for being unwilling to know us
only from a distance. You are not only God of this world,
but you are God with us.

Weekend Reflections

One of the incredible truths about Christmas is that God became a baby. Not a child. Not a man. But a helpless, hungry, crying infant. God came into our world, not in a flaming chariot, but through the womb of a young virgin named Mary. Such a truth gives us reason to call this "the season of wonder" and to celebrate the angels' announcement: "Today . . . a Savior has been born to you" (Luke 2:11). Take a moment to "wonder" about other wonderful components of the Christmas story.

Ripples of Reflection

- Why didn't God prepare a room for Mary and Joseph at the inn? Why was Jesus born in a stable?

- Why did the angels sing in the countryside instead of in the Bethlehem town square?

- Mary believed what the angel said. Could you have believed such an incredible promise? Explain your answer.

We Shall Be Like Him

We all . . . are changed into the same image. . . , even as by the Spirit of the Lord.—2 Corinthians 3:18 KJV

The more we see Jesus, the more we become like him. We reflect what we come in contact with. There is an unmistakable glow on the face of one who has received the Holy Spirit. It happens because the natural has met the supernatural. The temporal has encountered the eternal.

When we experience God this way, something happens to us in the spiritual realm. Oh, we may look the same on the outside. Our noses will still be in the same place, and our ears will be the same size, but something spiritual definitely happens. We are changed into the same image—his image. And we go from his presence reflecting what we have seen. This is the continual working of the Holy Spirit: to change us until we look, think, and act like Jesus.

The longer we know him, the more we should look like him, not so much because of what we are doing, but because of what the Spirit is doing in us. And this change goes on until that time when we no longer look through a dark glass but see him face to face.

Dear God, I want to be more like you.
May I hunger more for your presence
so that I will see your glory and be changed into your image.

What about Real Change?

We will hold to the truth in love, becoming more and more in
every way like Christ.—Ephesians 4:15 NLT

For most of us, change doesn't come easily. As Christians we want to change—to become ever more Christlike. But some days we wonder if we're making any progress because, when we're honest with ourselves, we just don't feel like we're changing.

If you find yourself in this predicament, let me offer some encouragement. First, the fact that you desire change is something to be thankful for. It is the holiness and purity of God's Spirit within you that isolates and rejects whatever is ungodly in you and calls you to change. This realization should bring about true humility and also help you understand that your desire to change is not self-generated; the urge itself is your indication that the Spirit is already working for change in you!

As we impatiently wait to change into more Christlike people, we may feel as if we are not growing at all. But we are. We look to our heavenly Father and say, "Will I ever be like you someday? I don't feel like I'm changing at all!"

And his patient words come back to us: "Do what you know to do. Keep my words in your heart; spend time with me and you'll see. Growth will come."

Father, help me to walk in your ways,
living the spiritual disciplines,
so that your Holy Spirit can transform me into your likeness.

Leave Change Up to God

Have I not chosen you, the Twelve? Yet one of you is a devil!—John 6:70

Changing other people is a futile, wearisome job. That is why, if we're smart, we'll leave the people-changing up to God.

Jesus was the best role model there ever was, yet in the end one of the Twelve betrayed him and the rest scattered in fear. Jesus understood that his disciples exerted their own willpower. He did not take it as defeat when they scattered. Surely, it hurt. But his confidence was in the power of God, the one who had brought them to him in the first place and who, he knew, would keep them.

This is a message of peace to the parent who is laden with guilt because a wayward son or daughter continues in a dangerous lifestyle despite the parent's best efforts to keep that child walking safely in God's path. And it's a message to lift the burden of the weary pastor who is discouraged by the low level of spiritual maturity in his congregation. It's reassurance to the wife who yearns for her husband to walk in the godly role he was created for. To all of you, this message says, "Place your hope in God, not in yourself. Be free from the guilt, the shame, the despair!"

God, I repent of trying to change people.
I give them up to you, the Changer of men.
Jesus, I pray that you "keep them through your name."

Growth Means Change

You will be changed into a different person.—1 Samuel 10:6

After the prophet Samuel anointed Saul to be the new king over Israel, Samuel gave him specific instructions. He told Saul to go up to the mountain where the Spirit of the Lord would change him into a different person. God could not use Saul the way he was, but Saul's obedience would bring about a radical change that would equip him for the coming challenges as king.

Children cannot become adults without going through the awkward changes that occur in adolescence. No one can bypass this stage. It is a requirement. It may be uncomfortable, difficult to understand, and downright humbling, but before you enjoy the rights of adulthood, you have to learn the lessons of childhood.

When you want to grow into a higher level of understanding as a Christian, you must be willing to change, and change can be difficult. In fact, it can be downright impossible sometimes! So the relieving hope for Christians is that it is God who initiates and affects change in our lives. We don't have to do it on our own. Real change comes as we let the Holy Spirit do the changing. "The Spirit of the Lord will come upon you . . . and you will be changed" (1 Samuel 10:6).

Lord, I want to say yes to your Spirit working in me, knowing that change will come not by my power but by your Spirit.

A Time to Throw Away

There is . . . a time to search and a time to lose. A time to keep and a time to throw away.—Ecclesiastes 3:1, 6 NLT

Are you one of those people who saves everything— just in case you might need it someday? Does the conversation on spring-cleaning day at your house sound something like this: "No! You can't throw that away. You never know when we might need it."

Some of us need to have spring cleaning of our minds. What outdated beliefs and remnants of guilt are lying around cluttering up your thoughts? What problems have you been avoiding dealing with? What dilemma have you been shelving, just hoping it will disappear? Deal with it! There is a time to throw things away, and for many of us, we're overdue! It's time to get busy. Rather than allowing something unpleasant to consume your energy all day long, get it over and done with. Clean your mental house!

For inspiration, read the story of young King Josiah, who became king at the ripe old age of eight! Josiah spent most of his years as king throwing away things. He cleansed the land of idols, false gods, and false images, and he led his nation into a time of blessing and consecration (see 2 Kings 22:1—23:29). He discovered the power of the "time to throw away."

Lord, you have thrown away all our sins into the depths of the sea (see Micah 7:19). You have set a time to throw away. I will follow your example.

Weekend Reflections

The end of the year is a good time to examine where we are in our Christian walk as well as where we want to be. Change is a big part of achieving our goals—not change for the sake of change, but changes that will stretch us in some way. As John Maxwell wrote in his book *Living at the Next Level*, "If you keep doing what you've always done, you'll always get what you've always gotten."

Ripples of Reflection

- What one change could you make right now in your journey toward Christian maturity that would be a major step toward reaching your goal?

- Take a look inside your mental closet. What do you need to throw away?

- There are some things you cannot change without God's intervention. What changes can you make that will move you into a position where God can change what you cannot change?